FILMS OF THE 1920s

Tol'able David

FILMS OF THE 1920s

Richard Dyer MacCann

THE SCARECROW PRESS, INC.
Lanham, Maryland & London

in association with

IMAGE & IDEA, INC.
Iowa City, Iowa

Printed in the United States of America.

Films of the 1920s / [compiled by] Richard Dyer MacCann.
       p. cm.— (American movies)
    Includes bibliographical references and index.
    ISBN 0–8108–3255–0 (cloth : alk. paper). — ISBN 0–8108–3256–9
(paper : alk. paper)
     1. Silent films—United States—History and criticism. I. MacCann,
Richard Dyer. II. Series.
PN1995.75.F56   1997
791.43'75'097309042—dc21   96–43027
                                                CIP

ISBN 0–8108–3255–0 (cloth : alk. paper
ISBN 0–8108–3256–9 (paper : alk. paper)

Library of Congress Cataloging-in-Publication Data

Other Books by Richard Dyer MacCann

A New Vice Presidency for a New Century (1991)
To Save Us From Ourselves (1994)
   A novel about American politics in the form of an epic poem.

Hollywood in Transition (1962)
Film and Society (1964)
Film: A Montage of Theories (1966)
The People's Films (1973)
The New Film Index (1975)
   (with Edward S. Perry)
Cinema Examined (1982)
   (with Jack C. Ellis)
The First Tycoons (1987)
The First Film Makers (1989)
The Stars Appear (1992)
The Silent Comedians (1993)

   Film/Video Works:

Degas: Master of Motion
   [USC, 1960]
How to Build a Freeway
How to Look at Freeways
   [L.A. County Schools, 1965]
Murder at Best
   [Feature film comedy, U of Iowa, 1981]
Quiet Channel series
   [10 Interviews, U of Iowa, 1983]
American Movies: The First Thirty Years
   [12 Video lectures, U of Iowa, 1984]
A New York Boy Comes to Iowa
   [Documentary, U of Iowa, 1988]

Acknowledgments

Extracts from Lewis Jacobs, *The Rise of the American Film*, reprinted by permission of the publisher. New York: Teachers College Press, (c) 1939, 1948, 1967 by Lewis Jacobs. All rights reserved. Pages 326-332, 396-404, plus extracts amounting to four pages from 404-15.

Reprint of interview with James Wong Howe by permission of the Putnam Publishing Group from *Hollywood Speaks: An Oral History*, by Mike Steen. Copyright (c) 1974 by Mike Steen.

Reprint of interview with Gaylord Carter by permission of the Putnam Publishing Group from *You Must Remember This*, by Walter Wagner. Copyright (c) 1975 by Walter Wagner.

Selection of pages 62-71, 83-84 from *Freedom of the Movies*, by Ruth Inglis, University of Chicago Press, copyright 1947 by the University of Chicago. All rights reserved. Published 1947.

Selection of pages 323-329, 337, 349-351 from *Memoirs of Will H. Hays* Will H. Hays. Copyright (c) 1955 by Doubleday. Used by permission of Doubleday, a division of Bantam Doubleday Dell Publishing Group Inc.

Excerpt from "Inventions Remaking Leisure" in *Middletown: A Study in American Culture* by Robert S. Lynd and Helen M. Lynd, copyright 1929 by Harcourt Brace & Company and renewed 1957 by Robert S. Lynd and Helen M. Lynd, reprinted by permission of the publisher.

Extracts from chapter entitled "The Twenties" in *From Reverence to Rape:The Treatment of Women in the Movies*, by Molly Haskell (Holt, Rinehart and Winston 1974). By permission of the author.

Excerpt from *Sunrise*, review by Molly Haskell, by permission of *Film Comment*. Credit on page 107.

Dancing Mothers, from *Classics of the Film*, by permission of the author, Arthur Lennig.

The Wind, extract from review in *Literature/Film Quarterly*, by permission of the author, John Tibbetts.

Credits for *Tol'able David, Manslaughter, The Marriage Circle, The Grand Duchess and the Waiter*, and *Seventh Heaven* may be found on the pages where they appear. Reprinted by permission of *Magill's Silent Cinema*, Salem Press, and Gale Research (Detroit).

"Miss Lulu Bett" a review by Tom Shales in *The American Film Heritage*, published by the American Film Institute, printed in Washington D.C. by Acropolis Books, 1972. Reprinted by permission of the author and the American Film Institute.

"*Show People*" extract and review by Tom Milne from an article "Davies" in *Sight and Sound*, Vol.37 No. 4, Autumn 1968, pages 200-201. Reprinted by permission of the British Film Institute.

"A Fine American Movie" [*The Crowd*] a review by Gilbert Seldes in the *New Republic*, March 7, 1928.

Photographs courtesy of Library, Academy of Motion Picture Arts and Sciences.

Contents

The Crowd

Introduction

The Culmination of Silent Cinema

During the slow, reluctant fade-out of silence from the screen (1926-1928), two motion pictures of singular quality and power came to stand like mute symbolic pillars at the gateway to sound. They rank among the best of all American films.

Like a good many other thoughtful movies of the decade, *Sunrise* and *The Crowd* were stories of women. Each, as it happens, was about a young couple—about internal strains on a marriage and the external stressful menace of the big city. In each film, a self-sacrificing wife is confronted by a husband unworthy of her, to whom she brings in the end a measure of comfort.

The mood and style of these landmark films were as different as their origins. *Sunrise* (1927) closely followed a script written in Germany by Carl Mayer, based on a story by Hermann Sudermann, announcing itself on the screen as a universal story "of no place and of every place." It was directed in America by F.W. Murnau, who had become foremost among the famous German directors of the twenties for *The Last Laugh*, an intensely gloomy story about a hotel doorman demoted to custodian. The silence of this film was so pure that it had, with one exception,no printed titles at all.

Murnau was brought from Germany to Hollywood by William Fox, who yearned to have at least one great prestige picture emerge from his studio. The sets representing the city were more costly than Fox could have dreamed, but he had his wish: *Sunrise* won three Academy Awards in the very first year those prizes were given.

The story is grim and simple. A peasant is so mesmerized by a woman from the city that he is persuaded to try to drown his wife. He makes a threatening move but cannot bring himself to do it.

When their boat arrives safely at the city, his wife flees from him. Only after a sad and desperate pursuit does he find her willing to forgive. Then it seems she has been lost in a storm on the way home: his punishment and purging are complete. Yet she has been saved. The ending is peaceful.

The concept is very literary, very European, and the picture is perfectly dominated by a style of despondency and fatality, even though lightened at the very last with an artificial infusion of audience-pleasing good luck. The shadowy camera work is fully keyed to the mood and philosophy of the story, and Janet Gaynor's pitiful situation is plainly visible in her stooped body and sorrowful visage. Many critics would agree that *Sunrise* is the most notable of the silent films made in Hollywood by the best directors from abroad—Erich von Stroheim, Victor Seastrom, Ernst Lubitsch, Maurice Tourneur, Josef von Sternberg, and Murnau.

Most of the movies by these visitors and immigrants carried burdens of cynicism, doubt, or inscrutable fate—tones of voice which contradict the characteristic hopefulness of the American dream, its expectations of self-help and improvement. *Sunrise* itself can be seen as one of the precursors of the wave of films called "noir" which grew to a flood in the late 1940s, although it is far more of a simple moral tale than those flashy fictions.

The Crowd (1928) was influenced in certain scenes—a hospital corridor, a rooming-house stairway—by the dark side of German cinematic expressionism. But King Vidor, its director-writer, was in unequal parts a Texan, a realist, and an optimist. He liked to try to make an ordinary man his hero. This personal documentary impulse brought him much praise and a long run on Broadway for his World War I picture, *The Big Parade* (1925).

Because of that great success, Irving Thalberg, executive in charge of production at Metro-Goldwyn-Mayer, allowed Vidor to go ahead with what was to be a critically honored and profitable but not a popular story. *The Crowd* seems to propose a commentary on lonely submergence or even danger in city living, perhaps a problem film in the Griffith tradition. It is more than that. It is a groping, earnest attempt to critique the American dream.

John is a young man who always expected to "be somebody," but finally realizes he is never going to "get ahead." The little family has some happiness, some tragedy, and there are wonderful moments of reflection on the common life in America. But the central figure is a man who is truly mediocre. When he wilfully, despairingly quits his job, we know (as does his wife) he has nowhere to go. When he applies for another position, he ends up carrying advertising on a sandwich board on a downtown street. The camera work, in key with the theme, is generally unsparing, cold, and ambiguous. It is a sad, honest, devastating story.

Vidor was not sure how to end it. He finally chose to have the family, after an uncertain reconciliation, sitting in a vast audience laughing at a clown onstage. Vidor's comment (in his autobiography): "John has learned to enjoy life, therefore he has conquered it." Yet to call the film a hymn to humility does not respond adequately to its underlying sorrows about false expectations. *The Crowd* is probably the most memorable and thought-provoking of all the dramas about American life by the best American-born directors in the 1920s—D.W. Griffith, Cecil B. DeMille, William de Mille, Henry King, Allan Dwan, John Ford, Rex Ingram, Frank Borzage, Clarence Brown, Herbert Brenon, Raoul Walsh, Marshall Neilan, and Vidor.

If we place to one side those motion pictures of the first thirty years which we have already chosen to prize because they were made by Griffith, Ince, Hart, or Stroheim, or because they starred Pickford, Fairbanks, Swanson, or Valentino, or because they were made by four major comedians (Chaplin, Keaton, Lloyd, Langdon) we are likely to come upon a number of titles which stand alone. They had authors, like those other films, but they were notable by themselves in achieving both popular and critical acceptance. They simply emerged from the busy crucible of talent and activity in the 1920s.

Henry King directed Richard Barthelmess on location in Virginia in *Tol'able David* (1921, First National). It is a nostalgic story of a young man's coming of age against desperate odds. His neighborhood invaded by bullying thugs, the boy manages to defend himself and deliver the mail his first day on the job. Shaped like a western, the story is eastern and local, yet universal, an early example of a long list of American stories directed by King, especially during the sound era, at 20th Century-Fox. William Everson, a historian of the silent era, calls *Tol'able David* King's masterpiece and Barthelmess' best performance.

William de Mille, Cecil's elder brother, directed Lois Wilson in *Miss Lulu Bett* (1921, Famous Players-Lasky), the story of a lonely woman's escape to a better life. Treated as a servant because she has to live with her sister's husband and family, Lulu wins our cheers when she is lucky enough to tell them off and run to the arms of the local schoolmaster. Few of William de Mille's films have survived. But we know enough of the stories he wrote and directed to realize that he was a special bearer of gentle humanistic themes on the screen, of very modest versions of the American dream. He was also a forerunner of such writers for live television in the 1950s as Paddy Chayevsky and Horton Foote.

Ernst Lubitsch, lately arrived from Germany, directed Adolphe Menjou and Florence Vidor in *The Marriage Circle* (1924, Warners), a comedy of manners teasing the idea of changing partners. This kind of sad and harmless sophistication served Lubitsch well into the sound era, culminating in *Trouble in Paradise* and *Ninotchka*.

Mal St. Clair, already known as a California-born director of stories of the rueful rich, became a competitor for Ernst Lubitsch with his light comedy *The Grand Duchess and the Waiter* (1926, Paramount) starring again Florence Vidor and Adolphe Menjou. When a titled lady in exile and her last remaining jewels meet an American millionaire impersonating a clumsy waiter, we are close to an experience of pure entertainment.

Other directors were reaching for genre identification. Ready to inherit the mantle of Bill Hart, John Ford (who had begun his long and happy identification with westerns when he directed *Straight Shooting* in 1917) gained his earliest fame in *The Iron Horse* (1924, Fox) a saga of railroad building.

The Phantom of the Opera (1925), starring Lon Chaney, while not the first, can lay claim to being the most impressive of a long line of horror pictures at the Universal studio.

Dancing Mothers (1926, Paramount) was perhaps the most satisfying of all those fictions in the 20s that attempted to redress the notion of a double standard. Based on a Broadway play, it gave Alice Joyce the surprising opportunity to walk out on her husband at the end, in the manner of Ibsen's *The Doll's House*. Joyce, Clara Bow, and the matinee idol Conway Tearle were directed by Herbert Brenon, a busy and talented man who was responsible for five other pictures that same year.

Underworld (1927, Paramount), starring George Bancroft, Evelyn Brent, and Clive Brook, was one of the first sympathetic portrayals of a gangster. Stylized in the highly visual aura that would later be associated with his Marlene Dietrich vehicles, it gained Josef von Sternberg praise as a director to be reckoned with and stood near the head of a future line of generic movies.

Seventh Heaven (1927, Fox) directed by Frank Borzage, starred Janet Gaynor and Charles Farrell. It offered the public an appealing young couple and romance achieved in spite of a depressing environment. It was followed by other popular films with the same director and stars.

The Wind (1927, M-G-M) was the Swedish director Victor Seastrom's vision of terror and fate represented by the oppressive storms of the American western plains. The parallel story, conveyed through the tortured figure of Lillian Gish, told of the tragic commitment to the necessity of loveless marriage.

Of course a lot more was going on in the 1920s than unexpected isolated masterpieces. This was the decade commonly called the age of jazz, and silent movies did the best they could to imitate the sound of jazz with actions, especially a dance with a good deal of sidewise provocative movement called the Charleston.

Women had finally won, by constitutional amendment, the right to vote. This was long overdue, but hard to represent visually. Tobacco companies persuaded many women there was pleasure in smoking cigarettes—that this was also an announcement of independence. The movies, to show women being independent, had them dancing the night away and smoking a lot.

Other kinds of freedom from restraints were being explored—and deplored—by movie-makers of the 1920s. Social trends toward frankness, frivolity, flesh, and infidelity were widely judged to be reactions from the unexpected carnage of World War I. Along with a malaise of declining faith in kindness and good will, there was widespread rebellion against the Prohibition amendment, which made intoxicating drinks illegal. The screen began to reflect this self-centeredness and lawlessness.

Puritan morality was on the defensive in the 1920s and nobody was more aware of it than Cecil B. DeMille. He found that audiences were interested in seeing the shocking sins and occasional sufferings of the very rich. It was possible through the medium of the motion picture to watch how scandalously certain accepted values were sometimes put aside. Exploring these departures generally took a lot longer than deploring them—a process of regret which might be briefly wrapped up in the last ten minutes.

DeMille was well aware that dramatic tension was conveniently served by current conflicts in values. Once he had spied out the audience's preoccupation with the attractions and dangers of sin, he held doggedly and with professional skill to this new approach during the early 20s. Many other directors followed his lead.

The "pre-war type of movie," Lewis Jacobs observed in *The Rise of the American Film*, "with its emphasis on religion, parental love, self-sacrifice, duty, devotion to home and family" was fading out and materialism and individualism were taking over. In terms of style, "refinement went out as aggressiveness came in. . . Love-making took on the appearance of a wrestling match."

In the American Film Institute catalog of all known 1920s movies there are 173 about motherhood, but 290 about infidelity.

In such DeMille movies as *Don't Change Your Husband* and *Why Change Your Wife?* divorce was deplored right there in the title. But at the same time divorce and even adultery were treated as common occurrences. And sex was proposed as a basic drive that might threaten a marriage from outside—but also, if sufficiently appreciated at home, should help keep home happy and humming.

Critics are never quite certain why they dislike DeMille. He was certainly a highly competent entertainer. His scripts were well constructed from a theatrical standpoint. His movies were popular, and he was constantly building a fresh roster of new stars from lesser-known people. It could be said that he met the subconscious desires of the democratic audience.

Do we shy away from approval because of his personal autocratic temperament? We know that he had a boy carrying a chair for him at all times so that he could, like an emperor, sit down without looking behind him. He was sometimes cruelly tyrannical on the set, enforcing general discipline by bearing down on some innocent actor like a merciless football coach. At lunch time he behaved like a king, summoning his staff to join him when he was ready, an entourage of nobles. When they all got to the commissary they sat on a platform a foot higher than the rest of the room. DeMille's oversize seat resembled a throne.

His sense of show business required him to seek above all things for public attention. He was ill served, however, by some of the publicity he accepted about himself. An advertisement in 1925 in Photoplay declared that his name was "written in letters of fire and gold across the entire history of motion pictures."

Even for many of his admirers, there was uneasiness about the relationship among sex, morality, and religion in his films. He started on the road to grandiose ancient stories by inserting historical spectacles, like parentheses, as parallel moral tales within his modern stories. It seemed clear that this usage of ancient times was to allow for more elaborate and explicit exploitation of women's bodies. By 1924, he was taking on full-length religious works like *The Ten Commandments*. But the biggest scene was not the thunder on Mt. Sinai. It was the orgy of disloyal worshippers of the golden calf.

Phil Koury, his publicist, remembers DeMille's easy response to critics who doubted his religious seriousness: "Read your Bible. I'm only giving you history!" At the same time, he wanted to be satisfied that the strong sexuality of certain scenes would bring in the customers. In his book, *Yes Mr. DeMille* (1959), Koury describes script conferences in which the great showman pointed out with earthy emphasis how sex must drive the plot.

Underneath all this was a basic pattern of thought which governed his approach to cinema. Many times he made the point to visitors and in interviews: "You must have evil in your story in order for virtue to triumph." This was a blunt statement of the essence of theater as conflict. But it also found its justification in the original philosophy of the serpent in the third chapter of Genesis: "Ye shall be as gods, knowing good and evil."

Evil was scriptural as well as natural and exciting. DeMille seemed to be persuading his audiences that there was some kind of virtue in viewing sinfulness, so long as there was a taste of punishment afterward, a masochism which paid for the thrills.

The sin in his stories was obviously intended to be attractive, but it often seemed to be flat and tasteless. His increasingly middle class audience went along with crime and punishment, all right, paralleling Calvinist assumptions—the fire and brimstone they were still afraid of. But they also felt, behind it all, a ritual literalism so easily dramatized that it gave the uncomfortable impression of parading around on stilts.

For D.W. Griffith, drama might be a means to moral advancement and, along the way, tragic stress and poetic feeling. In a DeMille picture, there was rarely any sense of delicacy. Far from the dogged righteousness of Bill Hart, and just as far from the cold pessimism of Stroheim, the DeMille aura was one of conventional holier-than-thou Puritanism—tempted, threatened, or deserted—accompanied by simple lessons of confession or hell.

DeMille was well informed about theology as well as theater. His father, although he had studied for the Episcopal priesthood, was never ordained, and he died when Cecil was twelve. Such an abrupt removal of parental protection was not unusual among the leading figures in the coming world of silent films.

Cecil's strong mother promptly set about starting a school for girls and an agency for actors and playwrights, including her own sons. In a few years, Cecil was collaborating on plays with the great impresario, David Belasco, as his father had done.

High church and New York theater: these were the platforms from which Cecil DeMille launched his career. Jesse Lasky hired him as a writer, then moved him to California to become a director. Always he kept the flair for getting attention, the sense of what a current audience wants, the commitment to profitable projects that were impressive and "theatrical." Always he was "on stage": a producer and director made famous by his own advertising.

King Vidor was in many ways DeMille's opposite number. Quiet and diffident, a behind-the-scenes kind of director, he was often attracted by the realist methods of the documentary film and the challenge of presenting characteristic problems of American life.

Vidor's roots were in Galveston, Texas. His earliest experiences with drama were in the cramped projection booth of a nickelodeon. There he kept himself awake by watching the actions and gestures of an early Italian short version of *Ben Hur* 147 times.

Fortified thus with the conviction that the essence of cinema was editing, he determined to practice by making short films for theaters—comedies, sponsored short subjects and newsreels. He ordered reels of film by mail, tracked down the actual owner of a movie camera in Houston, and embarked with him on a partnership. They soon sold profitable documentary news subjects: a major troop movement of the U.S. Army and a build-up of a hurricane.

Having fallen in love with Florence Arto, a local belle who also wanted to go to Hollywood, Vidor persuaded her to marry him and persuaded another male "partner" to take off with them on a trip across the southwest. He made a down payment on a Ford Model T and planned to sell footage of their hazardous travels to a newly created newsreel service of the Ford Motor Company.

King Vidor's father was a moderately successful lumberman, able to support such a venture. But the 19-year-old wanted to do it on his own savings. Like any cowboy riding a Conestoga wagon, he went west to meet his fate, and the three of them got more than their share of troubles—extreme cold, heat, electrical storms, gypsy crazies, flat tires, and also some equally surprising kind deeds. They slept in hammocks slung from the top of the car.

The way west in 1915 was via San Francisco. Once there, they had to pawn a revolver to pay for two nights in a rundown hotel and their first bath in three weeks. At General Delivery they found a check for footage of their first travelogue. They decided to sell the Model T. With these sums they paid off the Ford dealer back home, ate one big Italian dinner, and bought tickets on an ocean-going steamer south to where movies were made.

They looked up Corinne Griffith (a former Texan) at Vitagraph and with her help Florence immediately got an acting job. King began a much slower rise to prominence, first as an accounting clerk and then as a script writer at Universal.

The Vidors arrived in California below the poverty line. This is worth noting. They had braved the night and the rain, the endless pounding of the rocky road and the dangers of theft. They shared the lot of the common people. King Vidor never forgot it.

Compare this degraded status with the arrival, two years earlier, of DeMille and his star, Dustin Farnum. They came in on the train, well accoutered and ready to go to work on *The Squaw Man* for the biggest film company, Paramount. They had thought to get off at Flagstaff, Arizona, but quickly decided to go on. In Los Angeles, New Yorkers might expect more amenities of life.

Not till the very end of his career did Vidor take on the strain of big budget epics—*War and Peace* (1956), *Solomon and Sheba* (1959). Even these had a political and social edge that engaged his interest. But they were not his natural bent.

The Vidor works we shall remember as characteristic of his personal sincerity and his concern with the common life are those with roots in the documentary impulse.

In Los Angeles, as in Galveston, King Vidor started small. Doing a couple of days' newsreel work, he made the acquaintance of a certain Judge Willis Brown of the juvenile court, who had raised money for a series of short subjects. The idea behind the series was this: With the advice and help of the Judge and a few other fellows, a young boy in some kind of fictional trouble would be encouraged to go out and solve his problems. These dramatized case studies had considerable success in the theaters, and Vidor himself "deeply believed" in them.

One of the backers of these stories was a dentist who wanted to invest some more of his surplus funds in a feature-length film. Vidor, for his part, was trying to find someone who would hire him as a feature director. With eight other dentists putting in a thousand dollars each, he thought he could pay for a script he had written, *The Turn in the Road*. The only thing that worried Vidor was that there was a good deal of spiritual philosophy in the story—specifically, attempted answers to Pilate's question ("What is truth?") in terms of the healing works of Christian Science, the religion of Vidor's parents.

The good doctors were not at all bothered by this. They were aware that part of the appeal of the story was its religious aspect, its sincere search for a God who is good. As a matter of fact the serious subjectmatter and ultimately optimistic tone of the film attracted long lines of Scientists at the L.A. theater.

So successful was the writer-director's first feature in its New York release that the dentists asked him for more of the same. He felt obligated to them and made three more features, although he now began to have offers from the studios. Soon Vidor embarked on a busy career, sometimes signing up for pictures what would attest his ability to be a "commercial" director, sometimes searching out projects of his own.

Documentary realism and anti-mainstream religion: these were the platforms from which King Vidor began his career in Hollywood.

He was lucky in that his youthful career paralleled that of M-G-M production executive Irving Thalberg, who was not afraid of a bit of experimentation. Together they added a few high-budget scenes to a low-budget story about World War I, and *The Big Parade* (1925) played for two solid years at the Astor in New York.

With this motion picture, Vidor found himself, as he says, "among the top directors." He also found a favorite point of view. . . An ordinary middle class youth, carried on a wave of patriotic publicity, volunteers and goes to war in France, and we see the bitter actuality of it through his unaccustomed eyes. . . An ordinary character at the bottom of the heap in the big city undertakes marriage and family and then loses his job: in *The Crowd* we share his despair and his wife's sacrifice. . . An ordinary man, out of work in the depression, tries to set up a cooperative farm to help himself and others: we see his fears and hopes, in *Our Daily Bread* (1934, sound, United Artists).

With such difficult themes and unlikely stories, King Vidor established his place in Hollywood as the director most likely to grapple with liberal issues. His readiness to take on other kinds of stories kept his reputation understood as versatile: *La Boheme, Show People, Billy the Kid, The Champ* (1926-1931). Yet he kept returning to his preoccupation with the common people, making him possibly the most Jeffersonian Hollywood film maker.

The Jeffersonian view of democracy is an uncomfortable blend with aristocracy. Its history as an ideology in America has swung between support for the common people as farmers and laborers and support for the freedom of industrial tycoons. It is no wonder that someone with Vidor's limited education might find himself caught in confusions during his over-all career. His attraction to the idea of a benevolent co-op got lost in a final sequence of futile visual optimism—digging a ditch to bring water to the crops—in *Our Daily Bread*. His fondness for the idea of totally independent artistic freedom foundered in anarchism—dynamiting the architect's own dream—in Ayn Rand's *The Fountainhead* (1949).

Nevertheless, Vidor's constantly renewable enthusiasm and hope seemed to be rooted in a spiritual faith rare in Hollywood. He tackled the hardest human problems, then put his faith up against them. His protagonist in *The Crowd*, like Job, is afflicted with losses yet refuses to believe God would do this to him. (DeMille and Co., like Job's so-called friends, like poor John's overbearing brothers-in-law, would have said to him: "You must have sinned.")

The director himself, though not steady in his commitment to Christian Science, at least held to the view that evil cannot be God-given and therefore can be overcome. The notion of evils as external pressures, as problems of nurture rather than inborn conditions of nature, seems characteristically American.

Evil, DeMille would say, is inborn and inevitable — natural, sly as the serpent, menacing, ultimately destructive in all too many lives. Yet in *Manslaughter*, as in other modern stories, DeMille was willing to propose that reformation can follow purgatory. Individualist to the core, he could not deny himself the American moral commitment that draws on community pressure and human obligation.

Evil, Vidor would say, is something to be heroically struggled against — unnatural, crude, opposable, external. Mankind, blessed with a core of goodness and generosity, can learn to strain against the merely material view of inherited sin. Yet he found himself making for David O. Selznick, toward the end of his life, a picture called *Duel in the Sun*, in which greed and lust seemed all too dominant and inborn ugliness took over.

The evil is there, as DeMille understood, for the drama to use. There is historically too much sin in cinema to make it a dependable ally for peace, goodheartedness, and religion. If the film maker worships cinema more than he worships God, the Christian dictum holds true: No man can serve two masters. Cinema and religion are bound to be enemies most of the time.

King Vidor, like Citizen Kane, was straining too far, hoping too much for the medium he loved, when he wrote his "creed and pledge" in 1921 as an independent producer:

> I believe in the motion picture that carries a message to humanity. . . . I will not knowingly produce a picture that contains anything I do not believe to be absolutely true to human nature, anything that could injure anyone . . . I will never picture evil or wrong, except to prove the fallacy of its lure . . . I will endeavor to draw upon the inexhaustible source of Good for my stories, my guidance, and my inspiration.

The Vidor Village which bore this pledge was soon out of business and he went to work for other studios and distributors the rest of his life.

Show People was perhaps Vidor's most appropriate statement about human personality and class consciousness, placed as it was within the Hollywood scene he knew so well. When Peggy Pepper (played by Marion Davies) presumes to become a romantic star at an MGM-like studio, she discovers that her true identity as a comedienne is far more real, comfortable, and ready for romance. Moral: "Be yourself," which seems much like the Biblical command, "Thou shalt not bear false witness." But that's a hard saying for the performance arts and for cinema.

The Big Parade

Chapter 1

Some Special Skills

LEWIS JACOBS
Writers and Photographers

From The Rise of the American Film *(Harcourt Brace, 1939)*
reprinted by Teachers College Press, 1967. Pages 326-332, 396-404.
Jacobs was an early historian of American movies, and as such he has
not been equalled since. He did not limit his reach: he undertook to
deal with film as art, business, and social force. He read the trade
papers and went to the shows: he was there. This selection reveals some
of the richness of detail he was able to contribute to his history.

The day had passed when a newspaper reporter could jot down some ideas in his spare time and make money by selling them to the movies. Now that the technique of movies was becoming ever more defined and studio schedules were requiring more planning in advance, the staff writer was appreciated as a vital contributor to the business.

Samuel Goldwyn established a custom by engaging and widely publicizing such well-known authors as Rex Beach, Rupert Hughes, and Gertrude Atherton. Competition for "name" writers became fierce. Paramount was soon advertising that

> The greatest living authors are now working with Para-
> mount, Sir James Barrie you know; and Joseph Conrad, Ar-
> nold Bennett, Robert Hitchens, E. Phillips Oppenheim, Sir

Gilbert Parker, Elinor Glyn, Edward Knoblock, W. Somerset Maugham, Avery Hopwood, Henry Arthur Jones, Cosmo Hamilton, Edward Sheldon, Samuel Merwin, Harry J. O'Higgins—all these famous authors are actually in the studios writing new plays for Paramount Pictures, advising with directors, using the motion picture camera as they formerly used a pen.

Hollywood became the writer's Mecca. A steady stream of stories poured in from amateur plot makers throughout the world. Plagiarism suits became common; the cry of "swindling" was taken up. Soon companies refused to accept unsolicited manuscripts; only professional novelists and playwrights could now get through the closed studio doors, and "names" were esteemed as never before. Average prices paid to contemporary successful authors rose to $15,000, then $20,000 and up to $50,000, for a story. Stories were used up so fast that studios had to read books even before publication.

Despite their new recognition and high wages, authors were dissatisfied, declaring that nothing was demanded of them but a formula plot. Outspoken protests piled up. "As an author," declared Rex Beach, "I say that it is bunk that you want more and better authors. . . . What you want is more mush and slush, pre-digested pap." Such was the opinion of nearly all the famous writers.

Meanwhile it became increasingly clear that a good scenarist, rather than a good author, was perhaps the greatest asset to a studio. Photoplay writing had long been recognized as a specialized profession; the skill of translating plots into visual factors remained a trade known only by a few. No matter how famous the author of an original novel or play was, what gave the novel or play substance was its working out in terms of the camera and film. The ability to do this task was not easily developed; good scenarists were uncommon. Scenario writing demanded not only dramatic training but a thorough understanding of the film's unique tools. The best scenarists in the industry were not world-famous authors but the long-experienced motion picture script writers, many of whom had been working in the industry since its earliest days. In the words of Joseph Hergesheimer, "The moving pictures have learned to their sorrow that whereas a novel is valuable, a novelist is not."

The scenarists broke down the various parts of a proposed film story into the "synopsis," which outlined the story and then the "treatment," which was longer and developed the story from definite point of view. If accepted, the "treatment" was developed into the "continuity," which was a literary transcription of the finished movie as it would appear on the screen. This final form, being the director's "shooting" or "working" script, required a highly technical understanding of the film medium if it was to be of any real service and value. Continuity writers were therefore soon recognized as the backbone of production: they saved time and trouble in addition to planning the final form of the film, from which the cost of production was computed.

Though few scenarists became publicly known, their prestige mounted constantly. Increasing responsibility for the finished film was laid upon them. Often, in big producing companies, the director was given little or no chance to co-operate with the writer in the story's construction; in such cases, the real director of the film was the continuity writer. It was presently realized, however, that the best results were obtained when the director and scenarist worked together.

One of the most important scenarists in motion pictures during this time was June Mathis. To her—and to Thomas Ince—can be credited the make-up of continuity as we know it today. Gaining a reputation for her stress on timely themes and her careful planning, she originated the writer-director combination which was to plan the film's action before any shooting began. The result was less waste, lower production costs, and a smoother, more rounded picture. June Mathis proved that the carefully prepared shooting script was essential to good results in an art that was becoming more and more a collective project. As head of the Metro and Goldwyn units for a time, she became a potent influence on film making. Some of her best known successes at this time were *Eye for an Eye, The Red Lantern, The Brass Check,* and *The Four Horsemen of the Apocalypse.* She is still writing continuities today.

Next to June Mathis perhaps the most important scenario writer of the day was C. Gardner Sullivan. He had been an important worker in the Thomas Ince studio, where he had written, among other scripts, *The Aryan, The Payment,* and *The Pinch-Hitter.* It is said that the downfall of Ince was due in large measure to the severance of his relations with this capable scenarist. Sullivan is still a leading figure in scenario writing.

Other important scenarists included many who had become "typewriter stars" by 1918. Anita Loos was still a major writer, Her most famous film of the period being *Gentlemen Prefer Blondes.* Frances Marion, who had written most of Mary Pickford's vehicles, including *The Foundling, Rebecca of Sunnybrook Farm, The Little Princess, M'liss, Amarilly of Clothesline Alley,* and *Johanna Enlists,* was now known for her *The Scarlet Letter* and *The Wind.* Other prominent scenarists were Monte Katterjohn, editor of the first magazine for photo-playwrights, *Motopsis,* and Bess Meredyth, who, coming to movies in 1917, had written ninety features by 1919. Bess Meredyth is still one of the top-ranking writers.

Late in the post-war period others came to the fore, including such outstanding studio-trained scenarists as Howard Estabrook (*Driven to Kill, She Goes to War*), Jules Furthman (*Hotel Imperial, Underworld*), Benjamin Glazer (*The Flesh and the Devil*), and Sonya Levien (*Power of the Press, The Younger Generation*). From Europe came Hans Kraly and Carl Mayer, both of whom were the scenarists responsible for some of the most important foreign successes of these years. All these writers are important in their profession today.

Like script writing, subtitle writing steadily increased in importance. It was studied more and more, and many experiments were attempted. In *Mary's Ankle* (1920), animated titles danced to express elation. Other experiments took the form of large type, italics, and other visual means of bringing out the feeling behind the title, to make up for the lack of the player's voice. Toward the middle of the period there was a return to subtitles that were excessively literary, affected, and self-conscious. Lengthy and flowery phrases often approached the ludicrous. Even in *Greed,* as cut by June Mathis, there were many over-elaborate titles and bad literary clichés.

Two circumstances conspired to banish the fancy subtitle and bring back the succinct phrase. One was the foreign films, which had a notable lack of titles. *The Last Laugh,* in particular, was earnestly praised for its effort to eliminate the subtitle entirely. The effect of this phase on American movie makers was not lost: titles became more restrained. The other circumstance that reformed the subtitle was the change taking place in literature itself. The ascendancy of certain schools of experimental writers and poets, exemplified by James Joyce's *Ulysses,* was reflected on the screen. Observed *Motion Picture Classic,* in reviewing two of the new films.

> The syntax is sinful. Verbs left out . . . literary hiccups . . . inspired by a new school of experimentistic writing. Stimulating terseness.
>
> Something should be done forthwith toward bringing the subtitle back to normalcy. It has been taking excursions too much of late in arty pastures where the blunt phrase and the dot and dash live and have their being. . . . A good deal of the success of the Mack Sennett comedies is founded upon the wit of titles decorating them.

The duties of the title writer now were much more than merely the task of phrasing the thoughts of the players and writing "catch" lines and dialogue. It was the title editor, and the film cutter in a larger sense, who together worked out the final form of the film. It was their job first to assemble, out of thousands of feet of film, a story. This work required skill, ingenuity, and considerable tact. "Fill up the holes!" was a common order for them. It meant that they had to match scenes, to insert close-ups, flashes, and titles, to create suspense, to cover up plot inconsistencies, bad acting, the absence of necessary shots, and other inadequacies—in short, to turn out a smooth-flowing narrative. In doing this, moreover, they had to avoid offending the star, the director, and the author.

The duties of the film cutter were extended and made ever more important. Besides working with the director and title writer, often he was assigned to cut down the major pictures after their first runs. In the smaller towns the double-feature program had sprung up, and so the special features were shortened. Certain narrative adjustments were necessary, moreover, according to the locality where pictures were to be shown. People in some localities could follow action more readily than others, who had to see more of the details of a picture to understand it.

Among the better known cutters at this time were Rose and Jimmie Smith, who under Griffith had cut *Intolerance;* June Mathis, who cut *Greed;* and Dorothy Arzner, who worked on *The Covered Wagon.* Many of the better directors refused to allow anyone to cut their films, but in the rush of commercial requirements such an attitude was regarded by studio heads as eccentric.

Along with these marked developments in direction, screen writing, and cutting went developments in art direction. As a result of the invasion by foreign films, there was a renewed concern for decoration and costuming. It was quickly realized that otherwise weak stories could be made pleasing by charming the eye with color and the picturesque. Reviewers began to comment favorably on settings as they had previously noted quality in photography: "The settings are handsome," "Pictorially the effects are admirable," "Scenically interesting." Art directors and art departments, already established in the studios, were supplemented with researchers, interior decorators, furniture makers, carpenters, drapers, and fashion designers.

The problem of costume was particularly complicated. With picture fashions being watched assiduously by women patrons, the same gown could not be used too often in the same picture, and never in another picture. Styles had to be advanced enough so that when the picture reached the theatres, months later, the clothes would not look dated or out of fashion. Often, however, the remodeling of clothes could be done economically because colors did not have to match except in black and white values. As for the styles themselves, it was observed that clinging, draped gowns and sparkling jewelry photographed most effectively. With the camera and lighting facilities of the day, the problem of color and texture was also important. It was discovered that red photographed better as black than black itself; white reflected so much light that pastel shades were used instead to give the effect of white.

Photography was affected by the increased refinements of the camera, lens, film, and lighting equipment during these years. For a time after the close of the war, there was a vogue for diffused photography. Edges were made soft and fuzzy by gauze placed in front of the lenses, this being done to achieve the quality of certain paintings and for the practical reason that, in close-ups of women stars particularly, such photography was highly flattering—it softened features and eliminated signs of age. As lighting equipment improved, experience showed that proper lighting could secure the desired effects far better. Standards in art changed and the false notion of achieving artistry by making the photograph like a painting was discarded by the more capable movie makers.

The German school especially introduced many new ideas in photography. Their lighting schemes, camera effects, and careful compositions were slavishly copied, and their camera technicians were often brought to America to work on Hollywood productions.

Perhaps the most potent factor in the improvement of photography was the improvement of the film itself. All improvements in lighting and in the camera had depended upon improvements in film sensitivity. During the years 1924 to 1925 panchromatic film was invented and put to use. More sensitive to tonal values and capable of approximating the tones of nature closer than any other type of film then known, panchromatic film made possible revolutionary changes in photography, lighting, and settings. Less light was now needed, more natural colors could be used, make-up could be closer to normal, and the picture as a whole could have greater tones and brilliance.

By 1927 and 1928 the photography of American films had advanced so far and so rapidly that pictures a year or two old seemed greatly dated. Cinematographers numbered in the hundreds, the following being the most outstanding: John Arnold (*The Wind*), Joe August (*Two Arabian Knights, Beloved Rogue*), Lucien Andriot (*White Gold, The Valiant*), George Barnes (*The Winning of Barbara Worth, Magic Flame*), William Daniels (*Torrent, Flesh and the Devil*), Tony Gaudio (*The Temptress, The Racket*), Lee Garmes (*The Private Life of Helen of Troy*), Bert Glennon (*Hotel Imperial, Underworld*), Peverell

Marley (*The Volga Boatman, Silence*), Oliver Marsh (*Camille, Divine Woman*), Victor Milner (*The Way of All Flesh*), Hal Mohr (*Wedding March*), Charles Rosher (*Sunrise*), and Henry Sharp (*The Crowd*).

Seventh Heaven

JAMES WONG HOWE
Director of Photography

From Hollywood Speaks: An Oral History *(Putnam Publishing Group, 1974), an interview by Mike Steen, pages 210-215. Howe (1899-1976) became one of the most accomplished and sought-after cinematographers in Hollywood and worked into the 1970s. Unique in its charm and observation, his story is also representative of many other success stories of the time.*

They told me to go in the back gate on Argyle Street where the laboratory was and see a man named Alvin Wycoff, who was in charge of the camera department. He was also the chief photographer for Cecil B. De Mille. They were just finishing a picture which I believe was *Joan of Arc* with Geraldine Farrar. I waited around a couple of hours and was about to leave when the gateman said "There comes Mr. Wycoff now." I followed him into an office and introduced myself and said I was looking for a job as an assistant cameraman. He said, "Well, these cameras are very heavy to carry around. I don't know whether you can carry them," I said, "Don't worry about that. I may be slight, but I am very strong." He said, "I don't need an assistant. I just put a guy to work a few hours ago. But I can give you a job in the camera room, where we store the cameras and load the film. I want you to go down there and keep it clean. The boys throw these short pieces of film around, and they are very explosive and a fire hazard. When the time comes, I'll give you a job as an assistant cameraman."

Mike: These were the days before unions, of course!

Howe: Yes. You didn't have to worry about having a card to get in. It would be a lot different now. Mr. Wycoff said, "I can't pay you much money. Just ten dollars a week." I said, "When do I start?" He replied, "You're on salary now." I said, "Look, I'm all dressed up. I'm not going down there to be a janitor with these clothes on." He said, "No. I just want to show you the place and what to do. You come back tomorrow in work clothes." That's my introduction to a movie studio! I kept that camera room neat for about six months.

Meanwhile, De Mille had started another picture. They were shooting a scene with Gloria Swanson. She was in a cave, and a lion was to attack her while she was lying there. They had to have four or five cameras to shoot different angles and needed an extra assistant. I was sent to the set. My job was to hold the slate which identifies the scenes. Of course, I got a close-up all the time, by holding that slate! Mr. De Mille would see those close-ups of me with my Oriental face looking around curiously, and he was amused. He said to Mr. Wycoff, "I like that look. Keep him with us," So I became a third assistant cameraman with De Mille's unit!

I lived in a room in downtown Los Angeles, over the Third Street tunnel on Hill Street, for two and a half bucks a week, and took the streetcar to work for five cents a ride. Mr. De Mille used to come to work at ten in the morning and shoot until two or three in the afternoon before calling lunch. After lunch he would work until ten or eleven at night. After shooting I still had to work making up reports, cleaning cameras, and reloading the film. Many nights I'd miss the streetcar, which stopped running at midnight. Hollywood was like a little village. There were two hotels, the Christie Hotel and the Hollywood Hotel, which is gone now. I couldn't afford to stay in a hotel, and there was nowhere to sleep, so I would sleep on the set in Gloria Swanson's silk-sheeted bed! It was summertime, and the orange blossoms smelled great. It was heaven! The night watchman would come around and hear me snoring. He'd wake me up and say, "What are you doing here?" I'd say, "I missed the streetcar," He'd say, "OK. I'll wake you up, before anybody comes to work." He'd wake me about six o'clock. I'd go across the street to a place run by Mother Harrin and eat breakfast. A cup of coffee and two doughnuts for ten cents. Then I would punch in at the studio about seven o'clock. I got a raise to fifteen dollars a week, which was great!

Mike: You learned photography mostly by watching the cameramen at work?

Howe: More or less. I thought, if I really wanted to be a photographer, I should buy a still camera and start by learning how to take regular pictures. I went down to Fifth and Main in L.A. where all the pawnshops still are and got a little five-by-seven view camera. I practiced by taking pictures of all the extras and bit players. They didn't have agents in those days. Every actor and actress would have to leave pictures with the casting office to get work. I got so I could make pretty good portraits, which I would enlarge to eight-by-ten prints and sell for fifty cents each. I made more money that way than I did as an assistant! I almost quit being an assistant to become a portrait photographer, but Mr. Wycoff advised me to keep doing both. He said, "A portrait is like a close-up in movies. It's a very important thing to learn. All the stars, especially the women, want good close-ups. If you can make them look beautiful, they will ask for you."

Finally they promoted me to run the second camera. That meant, after the chief cameraman got his camera set up. I would look through it and see what he had. Then I would set my camera close to this and try to duplicate his view, his angle. The negative made by my camera was sent to Europe and was called the foreign negative. They didn't have duplicating film, so they had to send a separate negative to Europe from which release prints were made. It saved money to pay duty on one negative instead of on many prints. To be a cameraman I had to learn to crank. I couldn't take my camera home to practice, so I bought one of those little old wooden coffee grinders. I turned it with a rhythm which I counted, "One and two and . . . ." Film had to go through a camera at one foot a second. One foot of film consisted of sixteen frames. Today it is twenty-four frames per 2 foot and a half, because of sound. As a second cameraman I began making twenty-five dollars a week! That, plus my still portrait work, at times earned me more than a first cameraman. I also used my still camera to make background pictures for the subtitles. For instance, for a subtitle like "As time went by . . ." I'd photograph a sand hourglass in the background. The directors liked my work, so they'd have me on their sets often.

One of the big stars at Famous Players-Lasky Studios was Mary Miles Minter, a beautiful young lady with blue eyes and long blond curls. I was on her set one day, and I asked if I could take a few pictures. She answered yes, that she would be pleased. I took three or four portraits, which I enlarged to eleven-by-fourteen prints and presented them to her. She said, "Oh, Jimmy, these are very nice. Could you make me look like this in a movie?" I said, "Why, yes!" Nothing happened until a couple of months later, when I was called into the office of Charles Eyton, who was a fight referee before becoming studio manager. He said, "You've been doing very well around here. I'm going to promote you to chief cameraman." I was really surprised. He said, "Mary Miles Minter wants you for her cameraman." I could have fallen through the cement floor! I said, "Oh, no. I've only been here five years,. I'm not ready yet." He said, "Well, didn't you tell her you could make her look beautiful in the movies?" I told him about the stills I had made and that when she asked me if I could make her look like that in the movies, I had said yes. He said, "You've yessed yourself into being her chief cameraman. She's waiting to see you in her dressing room." I went to see her, and she had the stills on her dressing table. She said, "You know why I like these pictures, Jimmy? You made my eyes go dark!" We used orthochromatic film in those days causing blue to go white and red to go dark. It's the reverse today: blue goes black, and red goes light.

Well, Miss Minter's blue eyes went white on film. She said that sometimes her eyes photographed like glass and she looked as if she were blind. Now she was so pleased I would be able to photograph her eyes dark.

When I left her dressing room, I thought to myself, "How did I make her eyes go dark?" I racked my brain trying to remember. I walked back to the set where I had taken her pictures and studied the area. We didn't have the enclosed sound stages as we have today. We had stages with glass roofs with white muslin cloth under it. When we wanted to diffuse the sunlight, we'd pull the muslin closed. We also had artificial light, but we needed the daylight to help out because the film was slow. If we wanted to film for night, we had a black muslin we pulled over the glass. I looked around and saw a big piece of black velvet that had been used to make double exposures for a De Mille picture. I thought, "It must be that black velvet she was facing, causing her eyes to go dark. The eye is like a mirror, it reflects shades of light." So I got a little hand mirror and held it facing the black velvet. Sure enough, it was dark. I had a frame made five-by-six feet that I could move up and down and stretched a black velvet cloth over it. I cut a hole in the center and stuck my camera lens through. That was the way I made Miss Minter's close-ups! I kept the key light, the main light source, high up at a forty-five-degree angle so that it would not reflect in her eyes. The film was *Drums of Fate* in 1922. In Hollywood, the gossip was, "Do you know what Mary Miles Minter has done? She's imported herself an Oriental cameraman who photographs her while he hides behind black velvet, and he makes her blue eyes go dark!" Almost overnight I became a genius. Every blue-eyed actress wanted me to be her cameraman. I didn't have a contract with the studio, and suddenly I was being offered up to two hundred dollars a week by other studios. I went to Mr. Eyton and told him of these offers. He said, "Now, Jimmy, you're not going to leave us for a few dollars. We gave you your opportunity. We reared you. You're our boy. We'll give you a raise in time." He talked to me like a father and by the time he got through almost had me crying! He said "I'll tell you what I'll do, Jimmy. I'll put you under a three-year contract. The first year I'll give you one hundred twenty-five a week, the second year one hundred fifty, and the third year one hundred and seventy-five! And with a contract you get paid if you're on a picture or not, but you can't work for anybody else unless we give you permission. How's that?" Well, to me that was something! I signed without even reading it!

They worked me every day. I did the first film Pola Negri made after she came over from Germany, *The Spanish Dancer*, directed by Herbert Brenon. He liked my work, and I became his cameraman. When the studio moved to new facilities on Marathon Street and became Paramount Pictures, Brenon went to United Artists to do a picture, and I went with him. From there I went to MGM for a while and then to Fox. Later I came back to Paramount and still later to Columbia. The only studios I didn't work for were Hal Roach and Universal. That's how I went through the silent film days. We had fun in those days. The cameramen all had to wear their visor caps backward to be able to look through the camera. And we all wore puttees, because our pants leg would get caught on the tripod. On location we would only have an assistant director, not the huge crew now required. If the director saw a house he wanted to shoot, the assistant would knock on the door. If nobody was home, we'd set up our cameras in the yard and start working. The assistant would keep a lookout for the owners. When he saw them coming, he gave a signal, and we quickly packed up and hopped over the fence and ran. That was another reason for wearing puttees. We could clear the picket fences and not get our cuffs caught.

Mike: While moving from one setup to another, you carried the camera on your shoulder?

Howe: Yes, Cameras weren't motorized then. They were Pathe cameras which weighed less than thirty pounds.

GAYLORD CARTER
Silents Were Never Silent

From You Must Remember This *(Putnam Publishing Group, 1975), interviews by Walter Wagner. Carter played organ music during silent pictures, and his excellence brought him fame. Sometimes he had careful cue sheets that came with the movie reels. Often he had to guess from the first frame of a scene what it would be like—and modulate fast. He tells his career story with the same intuitive verve he brought to his performances.*

Before pictures began to talk his name and billing on a marquee — "Gaylord Carter at the Great Wurlitzer Organ" — was a formidable attraction. (Surprisingly, he is still a formidable attraction; the sound of the theater organ has not yet vanished from the musicscape of America.)

With a glissando down the keyboard, his instrument was sensitive enough to indicate a tear in Harold Lloyd's jacket; it was so powerful that its thunderstop could cave in a theater!

The surviving star organist of the silent era is a youthful, natty, sixty-one-year-old man in a brown Italian shirt and slacks. Five feet six, blue eyes punching holes in a sparkling, square-featured face, he lives in a charming beach house in the harbor town of San Pedro, a forty-minute freeway drive from Hollywood.

I grew up in Wichita, Kansas. My dad was a professor of music at Fairmont College. He didn't want me to be a musician. "In this business," he said, "there's a lot of prestige but no money." Because he didn't believe I should be involved with music, that I should try another career, he never encouraged me. I learned to play the organ and piano, I guess you could say, by absorption. I never had a formal lesson — if it's in you, it will come out.

I saw my first movie in Wichita's Palace Theater when I was twelve years old. The bill featured a kiddie cartoon and a movie called *Ondine*, which was a story about a girl swimmer who turned into a mermaid. I remember she was standing on a cliff wearing a gown that was blowing in the breeze. All of a sudden her gown disappeared. I thought, Oh, my goodness, she hasn't got any clothes on. It made quite an impression. I was hooked on movies from then on.

We moved to Los Angeles in 1922, and my dad opened a real estate office. One day a woman came in who had a theater for sale.

"By the way," she mentioned in passing, "if you know a piano player, we sure could use one."

"My son plays the piano," Dad said. I'd turned into something of a musician by then, and Dad was reconciled to it.

The woman said she'd give me a try. I was sixteen years old and going to high school. Though I was an avid movie fan, I couldn't afford even the modest admission prices in those days. Naturally, I jumped at the chance and rode the streetcar for an hour and a half to the Sunshine Theater.

At that time every theater, down to the scruffiest neighborhood dump, had some type of musical accompaniment for the pictures. There were an amazing number of full orchestras at the major houses. In the pit of the Sunshine, they had a thing called a photo player. That was a piano keyboard with a couple of small sets of organ pipes, and you could pull a stop and these little flutes would tootle along with the piano. The photo player also had drums and thumps and foghorns and cowbells. You would pull these ropes, and the thing would clank and bang. When you had everything going at once, the sound was pow, boom! Like the roar of an engine in a boiler room.

I'd play the supper show, which began at seven p.m. My baptism under fire was accompanying Marion Davies in *When Knighthood Was in Flower*, not exactly one of the all-time greats.

The owner seemed to like what I was doing, so she bought an organ with all the traps, xylophones, bells, siren, tuba, flugelhorn, the whole bit.

I was earning a stupendous fifteen dollars a week, and my hero was Jesse Crawford, probably the most famous theater organist who ever lived. He played all the great theaters in Los Angeles and Chicago and finally went to the Paramount in New York, where he earned twenty-five hundred a week, more than most movie stars — then and now.

What the organ did was punctuate, underscore, bridge, follow the action musically in order to add a dimension to the picture that wouldn't be there otherwise. Believe me, without the organ accompanist in silents most of the pictures would have been dull as succotash.

People forget that silent pictures were never silent. Even when they were shooting these emotional scenes at the studio, say, John Barrymore making love to Mary Astor in *Don Juan*, there would be a violinist or a string quartet on the set. The music put the actors in the right mood. So in presenting organ music in the theater you were just amplifying what they were working to when the picture was being photographed.

There was a different movie every night at the Sunshine. I never saw the picture till I got there. They would have what they called thematic cue sheets which would give the title of the picture and the musical cues all the way through. That was supplied by the studio. Each picture had a cue sheet which was delivered to the theater with the print of the film. Sometimes the cue sheets didn't help. I could always tell when the projectionist had a heavy date — he'd speed up the tempo of the film, and I had to do some very fast improvising.

After playing at the Sunshine, this little neighborhood house, for about two years, I got a job at the Seville Theater in Inglewood. Now this was a little better house. I had a nice pipe organ, a little larger than the one I'd been playing.

I'd played for Arbuckle, Chaplin, Mary Pickford and Douglas Fairbanks pictures, but the biggest attraction was Harold Lloyd. Instead of charging a flat rental fee, as was customary, he was on percentage. He knew his value, and he could make that arrangement because he owned his own studio and films. At the Seville, Lloyd would always have a representative from his office come to the theater to jot down the number of the first ticket sold and the last ticket sold, so in that way he had an accurate check.

The manager at the Seville would scream at Lloyd's price, but he knew if he didn't take the Lloyd picture, he wouldn't do any business. Still and all, the theater always made a profit on a Lloyd picture because Harold without question was the biggest business we would ever do there.

Harold and I got to be very, very dear friends. He was responsible for the biggest leap in my career. One day his representative apparently went to Lloyd and said something like, "There's a kid in that theater, and he's just kicking the heck out of the score. He's really making the picture do something." That particular picture, I recall, was *The Freshman*. Then Lloyd himself came down to see what I was doing. I guess he was satisfied. Years later, during one of my visits to his estate in Beverly Hills, he told me that he had mentioned me to the manager of the Million Dollar Theater in downtown Los Angeles. "There's a kid out in the sticks you ought to get in your theater."

Let me tell you about my first show at the Million Dollar. Here I was, really a kid from the sticks, flung into a *crème de la crème* atmosphere. The picture was *The Temptress*, with Greta Garbo and Antonio Moreno. The pit orchestra had thirty-five pieces. On the stage there was an atmospheric prologue with live performers and

Paul Whiteman and his concert orchestra. That night Whiteman played George Gershwin's *Rhapsody in Blue*. It was the first time I'd heard it.

The Million Dollar was a presentation house, where many of the pictures would run six months. A presentation house was something. The program would open with me playing a solo. Then the pit orchestra would appear to play the overture, and I accompanied them. This was followed by a newsreel and a comedy short, which I played. After that came the atmospheric prologue preceding the picture. The orchestra would play the first four or five minutes of the picture, and I'd be at the console for the rest of it. Then an attraction like Paul Whiteman. All this for thirty-five cents if you got in before four o'clock in the afternoon. Incredible!

Our biggest premiere at the Million Dollar was the original *Ben Hur* in 1927, which played six months and could have played six years. In those days a premiere was as big an event as a Broadway opening. Outside there were klieg lights and limousines and crowds, a bubble of excitement, of enchantment. Everybody would dress for the occasion, the men in black ties and tails, the women in stunning gowns. The stars of *Ben Hur*, Ramon Navarro and Francis X. Bushman, were there for the first night. So was the director, Fred Niblo. And Mary Pickford and Douglas Fairbanks.

When the doors opened, I was playing. Before I went on, Frank Newman, the general manager, who was such a fine guy, came to me and said, "Gaylord, the people have to listen to you for a long time and so just perfume the air with music."

In 1928 we had the premiere of *The Devil Dancer*, starring Gilda Gray. The picture was produced by Sam Goldwyn. Gilda Gray was a dancer from Poland whose real name was Marianna Michalska. She was credited with inventing the shimmy and was considered pretty hot stuff. She was appearing in the prologue, doing something called a fire dance. She finished her act with it.

That woman raised Cain with everybody. I remember the first thing that happened. When she saw her dressing room, she said, "Do you call this a dressing room! It's a pigpen! I'm not going to open in a place like this. Get it fixed up." So they put satin on the walls and made it look like a cushy boudoir. I never saw such a thing. I thought, Why are they fixing all this up for this tramp? She had a horrible reputation for promiscuity around town. She was a bum. Worse, she was an untalented bum. I can't imagine what Mr. Goldwyn, whose taste was usually impeccable, ever saw in her.

She'd watch her damn picture every night, sitting near me in a sloppy old dressing gown. She'd poke her finger into my ribs and say things like "Why don't you wake up?," "You're playing too fast," "You're playing too slow," "You're spoiling the picture." Hell, I was killing myself, and here she was complaining constantly. Her picture, thank God, only lasted three weeks.

I was at the Million Dollar for three years, and then I went to the Paramount. It was a tremendously large theater, one of the largest ever built, seating about fifty-five hundred people. The pit orchestra was led by Raymond Page, who later became the musical director of the Radio City Music Hall in New York. It had an organ that cost a hundred thousand dollars. The Paramount is now a parking lot, and that magnificent organ is in a pizza joint in Burlingame, a little town near San Francisco.

When Hope Jones designed the theater organ, he called it a unit orchestra, which meant, of course, that you had a complete orchestra in one instrument. And it could do almost anything, create a sob or a din like you never heard in all your life. It had only one flaw.

Those great Wurlitzers had what was called a thunderstop. A thunderstop consisted of a huge pipe thirty-two feet long, maybe five feet square at the top with a big reed at the bottom. The vibration it gave off was so powerful you can only compare it to an earthquake.

A friend of mine was the organist when *The Ten Commandments* opened at the Egyptian in 1923. He used the thunderstop for the scene when Moses receives the tablets from God. The theater literally shook and rumbled. The sound almost cracked the pillars. Hundreds, maybe thousands, of people might have been killed. Sid Grauman, who owned the theater, was so afraid of the thunderstop that he had it disconnected. In building the theater, the architect hadn't allowed for the thunderstop. I've never used it for obvious reasons; it was too dangerous.

While I was at the Paramount, the screen found its voice. The turnover from silents to sound was a wrenching experience for everyone in the industry — it just burst on us like a bomb. As soon as they could, the theaters let the orchestras go. And the organists fared little better. The Los Angeles *Times* ran a headline that read: SOUND PICTURES DRIVE ORGANISTS FROM THEATERS; MANAGERS REJOICE.

Pretty soon there were only two organists working in Los Angeles. Luckily, I was one of them. *The Jazz Singer* exploded in 1927, and there was a transition period which lasted until about 1933 for me. I played solos and specialty numbers and accompanied the newsreels, which were silent for a long time. And then I was looking for a job, too.

I went into radio and played for various programs. I did a show for a Los Angeles station from midnight till one a.m. called *The Phantom of the Opera*. I played spooky music, and it was quite popular. I got one fan letter that was addressed "Dear Fanny of the Opera." Then Amos and Andy moved out here from Chicago, and I was with them for seven years. I went into the Navy during World War II, and after that I alternated my time between jobs in radio and real estate investments.

About 1959 there was a revival of silent movies and a new interest in organ music. Suddenly I was in demand again, and I put together several shows, which I play in concerts all over the country. I've built up quite a circuit that I make once a year: San Diego, San Francisco, Portland, Seattle, Chicago, Kansas City, Denver, Phoenix, Columbus, Akron, and Cincinnati. In 1974 I was invited to Wichita and gave a show on the site of the old Palace Theater where I'd seen my first movie. There's a new theater there, the Century Two. I played organ accompaniment for two pictures, *Teddy at the Throttle*, which is about a dog that rescues Gloria Swanson from being tied to a railroad track, and *The Winning of Barbara Worth*, with Vilma Banky, Ronald Colman and Gary Cooper. That was Cooper's first picture, made in 1926.

I work with about twelve different movies. I've acquired prints of Buster Keaton's *The Navigator* and *The General*; Mary Pickford in *Rebecca of Sunnybrook Farm* and *My Best Girl*; Douglas Fairbanks' *The Mask of Zorro* and *The Thief of Baghdad*; *Ella Cinders* with Colleen Moore and a thing called *The Lost World* with Lewis Stone. Good silents are hard to come by. So many were destroyed or lost or buried somewhere in caves and forgotten.

Contrary to popular notion, silents aren't dead. Not for me and not for audiences. At some of my shows as many as three thousand people turn out at three dollars a head with a student rate of one dollar. My cut is twenty-five percent of the gross.

I'm astounded that half the audience is composed of young people. I did shows at the universities of Michigan and Cincinnati, which were enthusiastic sellouts. Many of these young people are taking film courses; some want to be filmmakers. Or they've read about silents or heard about them from their parents or grandparents. So they come out to see for themselves what silents are all about.

I'm not just saying this for the sake of nostalgia, but there was much about the silent days of moviegoing that was superior to what we have today. There was a certain feeling when you went into the big presentation houses that you don't get when you go to a movie theater today. For instance, you go to see *The Exorcist*. You wait around for a long time, you finally get in, you look at the movie, and then you go home. You don't get the feeling of grandeur you got when you used to go in and there was a great orchestra in the pit and a stage show.

The Ten Commandments

Chapter 2

Freedoms, Controls, and Images

LEWIS JACOBS
Films of the Postwar Decade

From The Rise of the American Film *(1939). In his landmark study, Jacobs spends quite a bit of time on Russian and German films and their reception in the U.S. as well as examining the D.W. Griffith spectacles. As an experimental film maker himself and a rather high-minded socialist, he didn't care for the new "freedoms" in moral behavior expressed in the 20s movies by some directors, and he lets us know how he felt. (Extracts from pages 396-399, 402-405, 410, 414-415.)*

The end of the war saw violent reverses in manners and morals. "The license of war time, trench coarseness and materialism, the sex life of great masses of young males held long without feminine companionships of the better kind, the atheism and pessimism bred in camps," to quote Fred Lewis Pattee, now bore their fruits. Changes in morals already begun as a result of the new scientific discoveries and attitudes were speeded by the popularity of Freudian psychology and the growing economic independence of women. The lust for thrills, excitement, and power, the recklessness and defiance of authority condoned by governmental policy, and a general social callousness due to the war, all combined to produce a moral uncertainty and laxity unprecedented in American history.

Two social currents therefore ran parallel at this time: reactionism in political and economic life and revolutionary attitudes in ethics. Belief in the old order of things having been undermined, idealism fell back before materialism; respectability and gentility became old-fashioned. Most of the post-war generation, impatient and bitter, wanted above all to be free of the old dogmas. Disdainful of anything that smacked of the past, they constantly rebelled against tradition and convention.

Restrained as life had been during the war days, it was now unbridled. Sexual promiscuity, faithlessness in marriage, divorce, bad manners, the hip flask, and general cynicism became popular as millions of people attempted to escape from responsibilities of all kinds. Americans surrendered themselves to fads and sensations: Emile Coué's "every-day-in-every-way" philosophy, the tabloids, the radio, Mah Jong, the Leopold and Loeb "thrill murder," Freud and the Libido, crossword puzzles, the Dayton trial, Florida and the building boom, golf, Eskimo pies, speakeasies, night clubs, roadhouses, bathing-beauty parades, Lindbergh, Ford's new Model A automobile, the stock market, Al Capone and gang rule in Chicago. All the while King Jazz titillated the nerves of the nation and gave the era its name.

Movies, like the Supreme Court, followed the election returns. They took up the cause of business, grew cynical, and participated in the repudiation of pre-war conventionality. Like the tabloids of the day, hundreds of films specialized in speed, spice, and spectacle. "Jazz films" by the middle of the period had superseded the last of the pictures in the pre-war tradition, substituting materialism and freedom for the old idealism. Popular directors of the previous era, such as Porter, Blackton, and even Griffith, could no longer satisfy the national appetite, just as popular novelists of the past — Hall Caine, Marie Corelli, Laura Jean Libby — were now "old stuff." These producers and writers were all moralists, and the public was tired of morality. People wanted to shock and be shocked.

Films attacked the genteel tradition with ever-increasing boldness, mirroring a nation that was recklessly experimenting, experiencing, asserting its right to live its own life regardless of age, class, or tradition. Hollywood movies pivoted almost exclusively on sex and sensation. Toward the close of the period the critical realism that had been evident in the works of literary rebels began to be manifested on the screen and to portend a change. The main traits of these ten years as reflected in films, however, were indifference to social responsibility and absorption in the "individual."

The reaction from progressivism was sharply revealed in film attacks on labor, liberalism, and Bolshevism. In the fright over the recent successful revolution in Russia, intolerance was running high. The business man's government unofficially enlisted the motion pictures, now that their war duties were ended, to do their bit in upholding capitalism. The government condoned Red scares, Palmer raids, race riots, and the expulsion of Socialist assemblymen in New York State, and sought to end the post-war tide of strikes in the building trades, shipping, stockyards and shipyards, subways, the shoe industry, communications mines, and railroads. At the same time it had the task of pacifying the men returning from France. A "gentlemen's agreement" was soon concluded between the national administration and the motion picture industry. It was reported in *The New York Times* for January 12, 1920:

> The movies will be used to combat Bolshevik propaganda as the result of the conference held yesterday. . . . Mr. Lane [Secretary of the Interior] emphasized in his address the necessity of showing films depicting the great opportunities which industrious immigrants may find in this country, and of stories of poor men who have risen high. He suggested that the industry organize immediately to spread throughout the country the story of America as exemplified in the story of Lincoln.

Movie makers earnestly set about to do their duty. Pictures painted Bolshevism in the blackest terms and declared that Americans would not for long ". . . tolerate or be misled by such foreign ideas." *Bolshevism on Trial,* based on Thomas Dixon's *Comrades* and advertised as an impartial representation of all sides of the question, was in reality a violent denunciation of the "impracticability of idealism, the eternal selfishness of human nature," and "the lunacy of free love." *The New Moon* caricatured the Bolshevik as indolent, lustful, cruel, vile. *Dangerous Hours* demonstrated how Bolshevism victimized everybody — the dreamer, siren, fanatic, coward, good-natured dupe, misguided student, bully, street woman, sneak, and old lady. *The Uplifters,* a film based on Wallace Irwin's book, satirized parlor Bolshevism. *The Undercurrent,* a variation on a favorite theme, told of the returned soldier who, "misled," becomes embroiled in "Red plots," only to perceive the danger at the last moment and turn on "the destroyers." . . .

The new materialistic standards and the rebellion against outmoded dogmas were first manifested on the screen in two signal "hits" of the blundering post-war year of 1919: *The Miracle Man* and *Male and Female*. *The Miracle Man* frankly and shockingly depicted the hero (Thomas Meighan) as a racketeer and crass materialist who seeks only easy graft. It openly acknowledged sex magnetism and the "sheer brute instinct which holds Rose to Burke." Such outspokenness and emphasis on sex were indicative of the new frame of mind, which dealt in "essentials." The exposure of racketeering, a new phenomenon in American life, with its exploitation of honest people for selfish ends, was in itself a significant disclosure of popular interests. Despite the spiritual note on which the film closed, *The Miracle Man* was a portent of the new, hard order of things in which principles were being discarded for material things.

Even more suggestive of the new era was the significantly titled *Male and Female*. A modernization of James Barrie's *The Admirable Crichton*, it related the intimate adventures of a lady (Gloria Swanson) and a butler (Thomas Meighan) on a desert isle, emphasizing the supremacy of sex over class barriers and condoning marital infidelity, "spice," and sensation for their own sake. More daring in its subject matter than any other picture Hollywood had produced, bolder in its attack on the genteel tradition, this film ushered in the new movie showmanship. Throughout it played on the audience's senses with luxurious settings, cave-man love scenes, sensual display. As DeMille, the director, pointed out, "The ruined woman is as out of style as the Victorian who used to faint." . . .

Wives became the heroines in all sorts of situations. Movies taught them to keep up their appearance and "style" after marriage, convinced them that they had a right to love and attention after marriage, and finally began to suggest that legal bonds should not prevent wives from having an independent life of their own — a prerogative heretofore looked upon as exclusively the property of husbands. *The Amateur Wife, The Misfit Wife, Poor Men's Wives, Behold My Wife,* and *Old Wives for New* all eloquently lectured on "the frump who learns it is important to remain stylish and good-looking after marriage." *Blind Husbands, The Devil's Passkey, Don't Neglect Your Wife, Foolish Wives,* and *The Merry Widow* pointed out that wives and mature women have a right to love after marriage and that business-engrossed husbands cannot expect to hold their "love-starved" wives. *Virtuous Wives, Flapper Wives, Bluebeard's Eighth Wife, Other Men's Wives, Scrambled Wives, The Married Flapper, Week-End Wives,* and *Miss Bluebeard* all mirrored the increasing daring and independence of the woman who engaged in flirtations and was growing ever more astute in using "her chastity as a fence between her and men."

As we already know, a new note in Continental sophistication and marital laxity was brought to the screen in the films of von Stroheim. These were sly thrusts at traditions and sentiments, and their gleeful acceptance by the public indicated how rightly attuned they were to the national state of mind — despite *Photoplay's* prim remark, regarding *Foolish Wives*, that it was "an insult to every American." Von Stroheim did not treat sex so frivolously as other directors; the underlying tone of even his lightest works was earnest. His insistence upon sex as a serious matter to be openly acknowledged rather than mockingly and teasingly exhibited was one of the reasons for the vast amount of antagonism — and praise — that his films inspired.

As the importance of love in marriage grew and sex became ever more predominant, pictures began to emphasize that disappointment and repression in marital relations (here Freud's influence was plain) were valid reasons for a married woman to have a fling at love and romance. Marriage became an open sesame to freedom rather than a responsibility. Elinor Glyn became the popular author of the day, and her novels were transposed regularly to the screen. *Three Weeks*, perhaps the most renowned of the movies based on her work, told the story of a queen who, bitterly disappointed in marriage, allows herself one romantic interlude. Hundreds of similar tales swamped the screen, thumbing their noses at "Victorian" codes as they justified adventures outside the bounds of marriage.

In the prevalent post-war disillusionment most people sought "escape." The movies obligingly offered substitutes for life in the form of exotic and erotic costume dramas, all affording vicarious satisfactions and extravagant visual magnificence. The phenomenal success of *The Sheik* (1921) climaxed the series of exotic "red-hot romances" begun toward the close of the war and started a cycle of dramas of the "great, throbbing desert": *Arabian Love, Burning Sands, One Stolen Night, When the Desert Calls, Tents of Allah, Sons of the Desert*. The men in all these films, were passionate and aggressive lovers who, casting aside all prudence, swept the women off their feet. Films of this sort waned toward the middle of the period as dramas in the jazz spirit became ever more daring.

Serving the same yearning for escape into dream worlds in the early twenties were the excessively sentimental and nostalgic adventure tales of by-gone days. Douglas Fairbanks reached the high peak in his career as a swashbuckling hero in *The Thief of Bagdad, Robin Hood, The Mark of Zorro*, and *The Three Musketeers*, being rivaled by the dashing Ramon Novarro of *The Prisoner of Zenda*, the heroic Milton Sills of *The Sea Hawk*, and the chivalrous John Barrymore of *Beau Brummel*. Sentimentally expressing the "back to normalcy" nostalgia were the sweet Norma Talmadge of *Smilin' Through*, the old-fashioned Marion Davies of *When Knighthood Was in Flower* and *Little Old New York*, and the endless series of films about imaginary kingdoms with imaginary kings winning imaginary queens: *The Bohemian Girl, Young April, Bardelys the Magnificent, If I Were Queen, Valencia* — Graustarkian fables all. These pictures catered to the public desire to forget the brusque, hard world of the moment in a make-believe world of grand romance.

Such story-book films grew fewer in number as the years of prosperity wore on and America grew more hardened and reckless. The farcical treatment of situations that would have been tragedies in pre-war days no longer appeared shocking, and movies had to become ever more daring if they were to titillate their audiences. Marital fidelity was now even ridiculed; adultery and philandering among mature married people were not only frankly condoned but made fashionable and attractive.

Lubitsch's films in particular were attuned to this attitude. In risqué and teasing terms his films all dealt with the flirtations and playfulness of the rich and carefree. His characters were always mature men and women of the world who engaged in their little games with full knowledge of what they were doing: sinfulness was now a spicy social sport rather than the road to a dire fate. *The Marriage Circle, Forbidden Paradise, Kiss Me Again,* and *Lady Windermere's Fan* were high-water marks of this movie fad. *The Marriage Circle* with its humor and its sophistication, portraying the promiscuity in high society between other men's wives and other wives' husbands, all engaging freely in the interplay, became a model for other movie makers and even for the national way of living. . . .

Marriage being regarded as a license for escapades, divorce was viewed as the path to even greater freedom. Divorcees and widows, like wives, were considered far more fascinating than young girls. The new pictures time and again showed divorcees victorious in their lives despite their unconventional position in society, as in *The Impossible Mrs. Bellew* and *Divorce Coupons*. Divorce was offered as an excuse for frivolity and excitement in such films as *On to Reno, Reno Divorce, The Merry Widow,* and *Beware of Widows*. . . .

The screen was invaded by hordes of "hot mammas," bathing beauties, and Volstead violators, as each movie tried to outdo its predecessor in daring licentiousness. Modesty and virginity became absurd as lovemaking took on the appearance of a wrestling match. The movie woman was now thrown around, carried off, flung on the couch by her man in the holocaust of primitive passion. Bedroom farces and other teasers were multitudinous: *The Gilded Lily, Lying Lips, Mad Love, Temptation, Passion Flame, More Deadly than the Male, Love Is an Awful Thing, One Week of Love; Parlor, Bedroom and Bath; La, La, Lucille; Twin Beds*. Movies glorified the smart set (*The Smart Set*), the Long Island set (*Upstairs and Down*), the country-club set (*Darling of the Rich*), and the "very rich, moral and very human humans of the Rolls Royce set" (*The Fighting Chance*). They depicted the *Wildness of Youth, Madness of Youth, Risky Business*; asked *Has the World Gone Made? Why Be Good?*; and captured the hysteria of *The Jazz Age, The Plastic Age, Flaming Youth, Reckless Youth, Our Dancing Daughters, Children of Divorce, Children of the Ritz*, and *Modern Maidens*. The sermonizing with which such films ended was mocked by the attractiveness with which they portrayed sin. . . .

As gangsterism became a more critical national problem toward the close of the twenties, an increasing number of gangster films reached the screen. They were now more realistic. *The Big City, Tenderloin*, and *Chicago After Midnight*, emphasized the fact that the complexities of city life make racketeering possible. *The Street of Forgotten Men*, in a tale described as "sordid," exposed the street beggars' racket. Josef von Sternberg's series — *Underworld, The Drag Net, The Docks of New York, Thunderbolt* — and Roland West's *Alibi* acidly depicted the underworld as aggressive and ruthless, as a plague in society. Lewis Milestone's *The Racket* attempted to expose the perfunctory activities of the police against the big city rackets with frankness and seriousness — an attitude soon to become pronounced. It is notable that the hardness and realism introduced in these films were to become the dominating tone in the next period.

The revolution in morality and manners that was taking place had introduced new ideals of personality. The modern girl evolved from flirt to flapper, to jazz baby, to baby vamp, to salamander, and finally to the sophisticated, colorful woman of the world. Wanda Hawley, Julia Faye, and Constance Talmadge were typical of "the young rascals whose bite was more dangerous because it was hidden behind innocent eyes" (*A Virtuous Vamp, Dangerous Business, The Love Expert, In Search of Sinners*). Colleen Moore, Clara Bow, Sue Carol, Madge Bellamy, Louise Brooks, and Joan Crawford typified the "frivolous, promiscuous, mocking type" with "a hard body and long, exposed legs, bobbed hair, bold eyes" (*The Perfect Flapper, Flaming Youth, It, Daughters of Pleasure, Get Your Man*). Gloria Swanson, Pola Negri, Norma Shearer, and Greta Garbo were the prototypes for the ultra-civilized, sleek and slender, knowing and disillusioned, restless, over-sexed and neurotic woman who "leads her own life" (*Flesh and the Devil, A Woman of the World, The Single Standard, Lady of Chance*). . . .

The critical realism of the literary vanguard was taken up by various film makers sporadically. Stroheim's brutally realistic *Greed*, Cruze's domestic satires, Vidor's *The Crowd*, Seastrom's sensitive *The Wind*, King's and Robertson's attempts at naturalism, and Chaplin's social satire were all significant. These signs of a serious concern with reality suggested that the broad social outlook that had been coming into being before the war had not been entirely lost.

Auspicious was the popular welcome given to the "documentary" films — factual records of man's struggle with his environment. The first of the "documentaries," Flaherty's *Nanook of the North*, appeared in 1922 in the midst of the deluge of "jazz" films. Its popularity was remarkable in view of the fact that the interest of the nation was at that time in escape, thrills, and personal sensations. *Nanook of the North* initiated a style for motion pictures which has only recently been revived with new vigor. Within the eight years that followed Flaherty's hit a dozen and more such efforts appeared in whole or partly fictionized treatments, notably *Grass, White Shadows in the South Seas, Moana, Tabu*, and *Trader Horn*.

The national craving for thrills, excitement, escape, and experience during the twenties was manifested by the tremendous patronage movies enjoyed. By 1926 the United States had 20,000 theatres, attended by 100,000,000 Americans weekly. The effect of motion pictures upon the very people whose desires it was attempting to satisfy had increased enormously in thirty years. When Willard Huntington Wright, the noted art critic, observed in 1919 that "The motion picture industry's staggering and far-reaching effect on American life has not yet been given proper recognition by historians and scientists," he hardly imagined what vast social territory the American film would yet encompass. In hundreds of towns the moving picture theatre had become the outstanding building — according to Charles Pettijohn, "a civic monument pointed out with pride by citizens, a place of culture where good music and good taste were being cultivated and reading encouraged."

Films during Porter's day, in reflecting reality, had made audiences more receptive and more reflective. Now films were helping people to forget, helping them to avoid reflection. Knowledge and awareness of the real world were rarely dispensed by the screen. Movies were framed to assist people to escape their personal problems, their frustrations, their unhappiness. The Lynds reported in their book *Middletown*, the classic record of the post-war decade, that movies quickened life for the

> youngsters who bulk large in the audiences, for the working man, for the wife and for the business class families who habitually attend. . . . At the comedies Middletown lives for an hour in a happy sophisticated make-believe world that leaves it, according to the advertisement of one film, "Happily convinced that Life is very well worth living."

The American film had thus become by 1929 a more powerful social agency than ever. Reflecting current states of mind, it also deeply influenced them. Its persuasiveness won not only natives of America but Europeans, Asiatics, South Americans, and even Africans. Hollywood, nationally and internationally supreme, was very nearly Americanizing the world. What Maurice Maeterlinck had said at the beginning of the period was, at its end, generally recognized to be true:

> . . . at no time in history has there been such a means of influencing the spirit of men and particularly of women and children. . . . All ideas of duty, justice, love, right, wrong, happiness, honor, luxury, beauty, all ideas regarding the goal of life . . . are ideas implanted by movies.

RUTH INGLIS
Early Attempts to Control

From Freedom of the Movies (University of Chicago Press, 1947) pages 62-71, 83-84. As one of the staff directors of a social science inquiry called the Commission on Freedom of the Press (appointed by Robert Hutchins, president of the University of Chicago, and financed by Henry Luce, founder of Time Magazine), Ruth Inglis researched and wrote this valuable summary of the development of the idea of "self-control" in Hollywood.

During the years immediately following the armistice in 1918 the young motion picture industry found itself caught between conflicting social trends. On the one hand, there was a strong tendency to reflect the rapidly changing moral standards of the times in the current press and theater. Sex was admitted to polite conversation and to the advertising, novels, and plays of the day. Picture producers were cautious because of their earlier experience with moralistic pressures, but the venturesome soon found that audiences seemed to enjoy risqué titles and daring scenes. Cecil B. DeMille became famous for his pictures exploiting the new morals and manners. Such titles as *Don't Change Your Husband, For Better or Worse,* and *Forbidden Fruit* emphasized marital infidelity and the doings of "flaming youth." DeMille's imitators were even less subtle, and pictures defying the old-fashioned canons of decency and morality became as common as the contemporary novels and plays in similar vein.

On the other hand, the loosening of moral bonds in motion pictures and in movie advertising brought the industry into sharp conflict with another trend of the times — a tendency toward the curtailment of liberty which had already found expression in the Volstead Act and a constitutional amendment establishing prohibition. Restrictive legislation was hailed as the cure for an increasing number of social ills. The evils of the movies were compared with the evils of the saloon, and the opposition to deviant moral behavior was organized and eager for another victory. Religious, civic, and women's groups swelled the wave of protest, and the demand for the reform of the movies became a national movement.

Critical surveys of motion picture content were conducted by many voluntary organizations throughout the country from 1918 to 1921. The study by the Chicago Political Equality League for the

General Federation of Women's Clubs was the most extensive and representative survey of the motion pictures of the time. Of the 1,765 films examined, 20 percent were called "good," 21 percent were "bad," and 59 percent were "not worth while." Although the data were crude and the categories subjectively defined, the results were similar to those obtained from other studies and were, at least, indicative of the content of movies just after the first World War.

If the content of the movies was objectionable, their advertising was even worse. Many people who never attended the cinema got their sole impression of motion picture entertainment from the advertising, which was often more sensational than the movies themselves. A sample of the advertising used by one successful theater owner reads:

Her Husband Drew The Girl To Him and —

A long, long kiss, a kiss of youth and love and beauty, all concentrating like rays into one focus, kindled from above; such kisses as belong to early days. Where heart, and soul, and sense in concert move, and the blood is lava, and the pulse is ablaze!

As Hampton, the movie historian, said in the *Pictorial Review* for February, 1921, it "makes you anxious to rush the kiddies to the show, doesn't it?" Another advertisement chanted:

Does it pay to love without question? If you are in doubt, love without question. Stop, look, love without question. All women love without question. It haunts you to love without question. It is passion that makes one love without question.

When words failed, photographs and drawings of women in scanty attire were communicative. Even the most innocent movies were advertised and titled on the basis of sex appeal. For example, Barrie's story *The Admirable Crichton* was released under the title *Male and Female*, and a movie based on the play *Du Barry* was entitled *Passion*. Both movie content and advertising reflected the lack of restraint of the times. As Will Hays stated in his annual report twenty years later, "None could deny that the lusty infant which was the movies had by 1922 transgressed some of the religious, ethical, and social mores upon which our society was built."

As we have seen, the movies were a new medium. The companies were still groping their way for content acceptable to the large audiences only recently attracted to the cinema. Mistakes were inevitable.

The reaction to the content of the movies was immediate and widespread. The General Federation of Women's Clubs publicized their 1919 survey of motion picture content and followed it by a demand for state legislation guaranteeing better films. The International Reform Federation and the Lord's Day Alliance actively promoted restrictive federal legislation. Religious leaders of all denominations raised their voices against the evils of the contemporary movie. A New York Christian Endeavor convention in the summer of 1920 condemned the film portrayal of ministers. The annual convention of the Central Conference of American Rabbis decried the demoralization of the drama and the motion picture. Other resolutions unfavorable to the industry were passed by Baptist, Episcopal, Methodist, and Presbyterian organizations. Editorials and articles written by those finding fault with the movies appeared in the newspapers and in such then prominent magazines as the *Literary Digest, Forum, World's Work, Outlook, The Unpartisan Review, Current Opinion,* and *Harper's Weekly,* as well as in the women's magazines and the religious press. Of the pamphleteers, the most outstanding were Ellis P. Oberholtzer, a Pennsylvania state censor; William Sheafe Chase, a member of the board of managers of the Lord's Day Alliance, and J.J. Phelan, a Toledo minister. The movies were under fire from all sides.

Weakness of the Industry

The industry faced this vigorous reform movement at a time when it was in a most insecure financial position. In addition to the effects of the general business depression, the movie companies had incurred attendance losses because of the influenza epidemic and sudden distaste of audiences for war pictures, many of which were already produced and had to be discarded. The large immediate profits to be derived from sensational pictures were too attractive to consider their effect upon the future condition of the industry as a whole. Most companies were reluctant to abandon this needed source of revenue. Indeed, there was little feeling of solidarity within the industry; competition was too keen for that. Each company and each faction of the industry were looking after their own interests, and each was quick to shift the blame for poor pictures to someone else. The exhibitors blamed the producers, and the producers claimed that the exhibitors failed to rent "good clean pictures" when they were made. A few boldly blamed low public taste. But there was no unified action on the part of the industry in response to the determined moralistic attack. In fact, the reform movement was given impetus by stupid publicity and the lack of a well-considered public relations policy.

The postwar lack of restraint extended to business as well as to morals, and in most industries "bigger" became synonymous with "better". The movie publicists were superlatively extravagant with superlatives. Everything connected with the making of movies became "stupendous" and "colossal." Industry costs, assets, investments, profits, and salaries were exaggerated even beyond their genuinely large size. In addition, internecine fights over stars and stories and theater sites among the movie companies and dissension among the production, distribution, and exhibition branches of the business led to bitter public accusations and litigation with its attendant bad publicity. It is not surprising that the public showed little faith in the industry.

The good name of the movies was further besmirched by an unfortunate series of Hollywood scandals involving movie personages whom the press agents had made known throughout the world. With the advent of the star system the industry had gone to great lengths to publicize the most intimate details of the private lives of its actors and actresses. When the ordinary attributes of life became commonplace in the fan magazines and the movie columns of the general press, unconventional marriages, romantic affairs, and divorces were vividly described. Press agents staged fake suicides and other hoaxes to advertise stars and pictures. Soon a substantial proportion of the public began to resent not only the fabulously high salaries but these tales of luxurious living, exotic parties, and the flaunting of traditional mores. When legal difficulties beset several Hollywood celebrities, the publicity proved a boomerang.

Mary Pickford had become famous for clean and girlish parts, and many of her fans were shocked when she stepped out of the role of "America's Sweetheart" in 1920 by divorcing Owen Moore in Nevada and immediately marrying Douglas Fairbanks. Shortly thereafter the attorney-general of Nevada threatened to rescind the divorce because of reported collusion, fraud and untruthful testimony. Although the charges were dropped several months later and today seem unsensational, at the time the affair put the industry in an unfavorable light.

In the summer of 1921 the Roscoe "Fatty" Arbuckle case became front-page news. The actor gave a party at the St. Francis Hotel in San Francisco at which one of his female guests died. Whatever the cause of her death, Arbuckle was charged with manslaughter, and the press implied that "a sex crime" had been committed. After several trials, Arbuckle was finally acquitted, but public indignation was so intense that he was forced to give up his film career.

The press of the early 1920's, itself not averse to sensationalism, vividly called public attention to the personal problems of prominent movie people. This was the heyday of the tabloid papers. The mysterious murder of William Desmond Taylor, an English director in the Lasky studios, is said to have sold more newspapers than did the entry of the United States into the first World War.

The dubious affairs of famous Hollywood people were supplemented by a stream of small scandals involving prostitutes and their friends attracted to Los Angeles by the booms in oil and real estate and who, being required by the California vagrancy law to give some occupation, registered as movie extras and called themselves actors or actresses. Hollywood became stereotyped as a place of drug, drink, and sex orgies.

The result was wholesale condemnation of Hollywood and the motion picture industry by all kinds of public bodies. The protests of professional reformers were supported by a large number of public-spirited citizens and groups who were disgusted not only with the content of films and film advertising but with the publicized conduct of movie people and the industry. With the cooperation of thousands of ministers, church members, club women, and schoolteachers, the reform movement gained proportions that became alarming to the industry. No business is more directly dependent upon a favorable public opinion than the motion picture industry, and its ill-repute with the public found expression in vital ways. Business at the box office declined, and extensive government censorship, regulation, or both, were threatened.

Federal Legislation Passed and Pending

At the close of the first World War, as at present, federal legislation affecting the motion picture industry was of four types: (1) copyright laws, (2) tax laws, (3) laws regulating the importation and shipment of films, and (4) miscellaneous laws regarding specific kinds of movies. The first two had nothing to do with the content of pictures. The Tariff Act of 1909 was of the third type. It provided that "all photographic films imported . . . shall be subject to such censorship as may be imposed by the Secretary of the Treasury." Because the number of imported films is small compared with the number produced in the United States and because the Secretary of the Treasury has never established rigid censorship of imported films, this statute has had little effect. The European film *Ecstasy* was censored at the border, but this was an exception.

The laws relating to prize fights and military uniforms were of the fourth type. In 1913 as a result of racial feeling aroused by a prize fight in which a Negro defeated the white heavyweight champion, Congress passed a law prohibiting the importation or interstate shipment of "any film or other pictorial representation of any fight or encounter of pugilists, under whatever name." Mainly affecting newsreels and short subjects and not infrequently violated, this law remained operative until 1940. A 1916 act and a 1919 amendment, making it unlawful to wear the uniform of the United States Army, Navy, or Marine Corps in such a way as to bring discredit or reproach upon these branches of the service, affect movies in which the United States military uniforms are worn by actors portraying villainous parts.

The foregoing legislation constituted the only sources of federal control over motion picture content which existed at the time. Proposals for federal censorship, however, were an old problem. In 1915 a bill was introduced in Congress providing for a Federal Motion Picture Commission as a division of the Bureau of Education in the Department of the Interior. A commission of five members appointed by the President of the United States was to examine, censor, and license all films before they could be admitted to interstate commerce. After extensive hearings, the bill was defeated. Although almost every subsequent session of Congress had seen similar bills, they were not a serious threat to the industry until about 1920.

In an effort to avert federal censorship and to place motion pictures clearly on an equal basis with newspapers, magazines, and books as far as federal control of content was concerned, the National Association of the Motion Picture Industry, a precursor of the Hays Office, had sponsored two changes in the federal statutes. The first, an amendment to the Constitution providing for the freedom of the screen, made no progress whatever. The second, a revision of section 245 of the *United States Penal Code* to include movies with other matter which may not be imported or transported by any common carrier in interstate commerce if it is obscene, lewd, lascivious, filthy, or of indecent character, was passed by Congress in June, 1920. But it brought no tangible improvement, and the demand for federal control of the movies continued unabated.

Several measures were proposed in Congress. In 1920 both the Senate and the House of Representatives entertained bills designed to prevent the exhibition of movies showing "the acts and conduct of ex-convicts, desperadoes, bandits, train robbers, bank robbers, or outlaws in the commission or attempted commission of crime or acts of violence." Senator Henry L. Myers of South Dakota in August, 1921, sponsored a resolution calling for a congressional investigation of the motion picture industry. During the following winter two separate motion picture censorship bills were introduced into the lower house.

The industry successfully fought all these measures, but the pressure for federal legislation was becoming alarmingly stronger each year.

State, Municipal, and Foreign Legislation

Meanwhile, censorship was being debated in other places, domestic and foreign. During 1921 nearly one hundred measures relative to the movies were introduced in the legislatures of thirty-seven states. Several states and a good many municipalities already had enacted restrictive motion picture legislation. Chicago led the way in 1907, and Pennsylvania followed in 1911 with a law which became operative in 1913. The Pennsylvania law set the pattern which was followed by most of the states in which censorship laws were enacted or proposed. It created the Pennsylvania State Board of Censors composed of three persons, two men and one woman, who are appointed by the governor for a term of three years at salaries of $3,000 for the chairman, $2,500 for the vice-chairman, and $2,400 for the secretary. No film can be sold, leased, lent, or exhibited in the state unless it has been submitted to, and approved by, this board of censors. A fee of $2.00 is charged for each 1,200 feet of film inspected. All advertising material must also be submitted and approved. Ohio and Kansas passed similar laws in 1913, the Ohio censors, however, serving without pay. Most censors are political appointees.

The validity of the Chicago ordinance and the three state laws was contested in the courts, the contention being that they violated the provision in the Bill of Rights guaranteeing freedom of speech and the constitutional requirement of "due process of law." The courts, however, sustained all three laws as being a reasonable exercise of state police power, the cases involving the Pennsylvania, Ohio, and Kansas statutes being carried to the United States Supreme Court during 1915. . . .

Producers found it difficult to predict the reactions of the censor boards. The result was that the post-production cuts frequently destroyed the continuity of pictures or made it difficult for the audience to follow the plot of the story. After the first World War, as the number of cuts and rejections increased, the problem became correspondingly acute. Because of this difficulty and the strong agitation for additional state censoring bodies, many of the producers, resigning themselves to the inevitability of some kind of censorship, favored federal censorship as a lesser evil than multiform state boards and rules — meanwhile, however, opposing the specific bills before Congress. . . .

National Association of the Motion Picture Industry

In April, 1919, as was noted above, the National Association of the Motion Picture Industry sponsored not only an amendment to the penal law which was adopted but also an amendment to the Constitution of the United States providing for freedom of the screen. The latter proposal was quashed in congressional committee. At the same time the Association's president, William A. Brady, suggested that the Association itself censor films and that members refuse to rent any pictures to exhibitors who showed films of which the Association disapproved. This suggested plan of self-regulation did not materialize immediately; in fact, nothing more was heard of it until March 7, 1921, when the National Association announced the establishment of the "Thirteen Points".

These Thirteen Points were a series of resolutions specifically condemning the production and exhibition of certain kinds of pictures to which objection was taken and which were being most frequently cut by the existing censor boards. They were pictures

1. Which emphasize and exaggerate sex appeal or depict scenes therein exploiting interest in sex in an improper or suggestive form or manner

2. Based upon white slavery or commercialized vice or scenes showing the procurement of women or any of the activities attendant upon this traffic

3. Thematically making prominent an illicit love affair which tends to make virtue odious and vice attractive

4. With scenes which exhibit nakedness or persons scantily dressed, particularly suggestive bedroom and bathroom scenes and scenes of inciting dancing

5. With scenes which unnecessarily prolong expressions or demonstrations of passionate love

6. Predominantly concerned with the underworld or vice and crime, and like scenes, unless the scenes are part of an essential conflict between good and evil

7. Of stories which make gambling and drunkenness attractive, or of scenes which show the use of narcotics and other unnatural practices dangerous to social morality

8. Of stories and scenes which may instruct the morally feeble in methods of committing crimes, or, by cumulative processes, emphasize crime and the commission of crime

9. Of stories or scenes which ridicule or deprecate public officials, officers of the law, the United States Army, the United States Navy, or other governmental authority, or which tend to weaken the authority of the law

10. Of stories or scenes or incidents which offend religious belief or any person, creed or sect, or ridicule ministers, priests, rabbis or recognized leaders of any religious sect, and also which are disrespectful to objects or symbols used in connection with any religion

11. Of stories or with scenes which unduly emphasize bloodshed and violence without justification in the structure of the story

12. Of stories or with scenes which are vulgar and portray improper gestures, posturing, and attitudes

13. With salacious titles and subtitles in connection with their presentation or exhibition, and the use of salacious advertising matter, photographs, and lithographs in connection therewith . . .

If the Thirteen Points had been intelligently enforced, most of the industry's troubles with public groups during the following fifteen years might have been averted. At least one influential group, the National Catholic Welfare Council, was willing to cooperate with the industry on this basis. . . .

The National Association of the Motion Picture Industry, however, established no machinery for putting its good resolutions into effect. The fact was that it was unable to do so. The Association lacked both the financial and the moral support of the industry necessary to make it effective. Nevertheless, President William A. Brady did his best to publicize the Thirteen Points and to stem the rising demand for censorship. . . .

WILL H. HAYS
The First Year in Hollywood, 1922-1923

From The Memoirs of Will H. Hays *(Garden City, N.Y., Doubleday & Co., 1955) pages 323-329, 337, 349-351. When the owners of the major motion picture companies began to be squeezed between the desires of one part of the public for movies without restraints and another part of the public for more restraints on the movies, they were lucky enough to find a Presbyterian elder who believed that a middle way could be sold to both sides. In his personal story, rarely read by film students, he explains how he saw his mission and how reasonable it seemed to him to try to serve the real needs of Hollywood's audience.*

It was because of the peculiar character of my professional life, dealing so largely with mass movements and popular forces — like those in national politics and in international motion pictures — that the publishers of this volume asked me to set down some of these experiences and observations, with my personal interpretation of some of the changes that have taken place. They seemed to feel that such a recital, telling a story that leads from Sullivan, Indiana, around the world and back, might shed light on some of the ways in which public opinion and public action may be directed into wholesome channels.

Perhaps the greatest lesson I have learned is that *it is possible to change public opinion, to marshal it behind constructive projects* like woman suffrage or clean movies. Two indispensable factors are a sound plan and a vigorous organization for winning the cooperation of right-thinking men and women. One of the surest, simplest policies is always to *seek points of agreement*, not points of difference. These convictions I have voiced over and over in such slogans as "Things don't happen — they are brought about"; and "Whatever ought to be done is doable."

I have no corner on such a philosophy of life. It has animated the whole vigorous pioneering spirit of millions of Americans. Perhaps it seemed to burn with unusual fervor in such sections as the Midwest "Valley of Democracy," where faith in our homes, our friends and neighbors, our state, our nation, and our God seemed as natural as the air we breathed.

Years ago I wrote a magazine article entitled "I Learned a Lot from the Folks Back Home." This book tries to tell the story — or many stories — of how I have seen this typically American philosophy of life at work. In a real sense, it is the story of thousands of men and women with whom it has been my privilege and joy to associate, through more than half a century, in projects that seemed to us worth while.

Had an Aladdin's genie appeared to me as I left New York on the fateful trip that was also to include a train accident, and had he told me that in a few days I would be offered the post of "czar" of the motion picture industry, I surely would have thought it a fairy tale. My astonishment was utter and complete when, on the eighth day of December, 1921, Saul Rogers and Lewis J. Selznick asked to see me in my suite at the Wardman Park Hotel.

I was still convalescing from injuries sustained in the train wreck, and I had never met either man before. My first impulse was to beg off the interview, which I thought vaguely must have to do with some motion picture problem of the Post Office Department. Surely this could wait. Yet, to be consistent with the "open door" policy I had already established, and since I did not think I was honestly too ill to receive visitors, I consented.

Mr. Rogers and Mr. Selznick came straight to the point. They handed me a round-robin letter signed by ten of the leading motion picture producers and by officers of two additional companies, asking me to become head of the Association they felt it urgently necessary to form. There had been a previous association under the presidency of the illustrious producer, William A. Brady, but this had become useless owing to lack of agreement among its members. In the face of pressing problems, a comprehensive and definite program was now being sought.

Beyond the fact that I had arranged for the newsreels to have proportionate coverage with the press during the campaign, I had never been identified with any phase of motion pictures. I was just an Indiana lawyer who had become Republican national chairman, then Postmaster General. Just that. I was aware, of course, of a certain ferment going on in the industry and of increasing tension between the industry and some influential sections of the public. As happens in the history of every institution, human frailty had ushered in by degrees what appeared to many to be an era of scandal. This had even happened in our wholesome national game of baseball and had resulted in the selection of Judge Kenesaw M. Landis as an over-all commissioner, or "czar," as he was usually called. And recently in Hollywood there had occurred a series of unsavory incidents which had given the responsible-minded pro-

ducers as much concern in their capacity as good citizens as in their
professional status as picture-makers. I am sure these considerations influenced the producers and distributors in their decision to
follow the lead of baseball.

The question still remained in my mind: why me?

Rogers and Selznick spoke sincerely and in a highly complimen-
tary way, but I did not feel that their reasons for selecting me were
justified. Since then I have read a number of rationalizations, in
articles and books, setting forth what my qualifications might have
been. These still strike me as more flattering than convincing. However, there it was. I promised to think it over during the Christmas
holidays.

As it turned out, "thinking it over" proved to be a big job, at any
rate subjectively. In this case I was not only trying to decide something but to weigh and analyze my own inner motive. I knew that
if I accepted the offer I would be criticized for yielding to a merce-
nary object and renouncing, as it were, dignity for gain — as if being
Postmaster General were something priestly, consecrated by vows
which a man might not forsake with self-respect. I realized that such
a view was simply dramatizing the matter; neither did it take into
account my previously formed determination to return to private
life as soon as I could, as I had told President Harding before his
inauguration. It was understood that I would remain as Postmaster
General only until the department was satisfactorily reorganized,
and I felt that this had been accomplished.

I chuckle now at my fancy that the motion picture post would
signify any kind of "private life."

There was another side to the problem I had to consider. I had
been raised in a Christian home, and while I am not a reformer I
hope that I have always been public-spirited. It required no great
insight to see that the young movie giant might well grow up a
Frankenstein. And precisely because I was not a reformer, I dreaded
the blunders the reformers would make in dealing with this new
and vital force. I was thinking of the parallel case of prohibition —
which had by no means produced the era of national sobriety its
proponents had contemplated.

For the moment I did not confide my problem to anyone. In a few
days I would join my home folks in Sullivan. I had recovered
sufficiently to attend to some routine matters preparatory to leaving
when, to my dismay, the story of the offer broke in the press.
Certainly I had given no indication of the business, even to intimate
friends. I had wanted to think it out by myself. I knew, too, without
having to be reassured, that neither Mr. Selznick, Mr. Rogers, nor

any of their associates would wish to break the story prematurely. But it had leaked out, and it proved embarrassing. One newspaper went so far as to declare that I had flatly rejected the offer, which was news to me.

I was promptly beleaguered by callers and subjected to a barrage of messages from well-wishers, reporters, feature writers, and persons whom I had never met but who had free advice to give. There was also a lunatic fringe of those who wanted some jobs in the movies, for themselves or for some talented brother-in-law, and who demanded that I use my mystic power to place them.

While I was still upset physically and mentally, Courtland Smith came to my rescue. He not only shielded me from the more importunate inquisitors but, perceiving that I was almost at the breaking point, forced me to take long walks with him through Rock Creek Park. It was December, and there was a wild and dismal beauty to many of its vistas which might have affected a more melancholy temperament adversely but which I found extremely relaxing. It seemed as if I were a million miles from the turmoil of telephone calls, questions, criticism, and flattery that the leak to the press had brought down about my ears.

Finally it was Courtland who decided I should get out of Washington earlier than planned and make what might be called, in a certain sense, a retreat. My hideaway for this purpose was the home of my great and good friend Colonel William Boyce Thompson, at Yonkers, New York. I had sought his counsel on many previous occasions and valued it highly. This time he insisted that I take it easy, so literally that I spent the first few days in bed in a darkened room and was not even allowed to look at newspapers. I never knew a more kindly or solicitous host than Bill Thompson.

On Christmas Day in Sullivan I made up my mind. As I was sitting at breakfast, I overheard an argument in the next room. My boy Bill, who was six, and his two cousins, Charles and John, a little older and a little younger, were putting on the cowboy suits I had bought them.

"I want to be William S. Hart!" cried my boy.

"No, I'm going to be him!" contradicted one of my nephews.

"No, I am! You can be Doug, and Bill can be the bad guy," yelled the other.

The text from Scripture, "Out of the mouths of babes and sucklings Thou has perfected praise" flashed through my mind. They wanted to be Bill Hart. Not Buffalo Bill. Not Daniel Boone. But William S. Hart! To these little boys and to thousands of others throughout our land, William S. Hart and Mary and Doug were real and important personages and, at least in their screen characters, models of character and behavior. And I may interject that if all of the pictures produced in Hollywood had been as wholesome as those in which Bill Hart, Mary Pickford, and Douglas Fairbanks appeared there would never have been such a storm of public protest as developed.

I realized on that Christmas morning that motion pictures had become as strong an influence on our children and on countless adults, too, as the daily press. The juvenile argument which I had overheard confirmed my feeling and my fears that the great motion picture industry might as easily become a corrupting as a beneficial influence on our future generations.

At any rate, this was the thing that crystallized my decision. And when some months later I related the incident to Bill Hart, he was deeply affected and the following Christmas sent my boy the bridle he had used in many pictures.

Now that I had made up my mind, it was up to me to think out my philosophy of the job I had been called upon to do. The Christmas respite came to an end all too quickly, and on January 2, 1922, I was in New York on my way back to Washington. Interviewed by the papers, I stated that I would meet the motion picture producers on January 14, which I subsequently did.

Meanwhile, I had already become the target for the fusillade of criticism I had anticipated. My friend Senator Pat Harrison of Mississippi felt that a Cabinet officer had no business resigning his high office for an amusement-industry post. Henry Ford, who I am sure meant well, gave vent to his distress in his Dearborn *Independent*. Dr. Wilbur Crafts, an eminent divine, charged that I had been "bought."

The tenor of most of the criticism seemed to be that I was hiring myself out to the motion picture interests as a sort of "fixer," to shield them from public and possibly legislative wrath. This notion on the part of the champions of decency became especially articulate when they discovered that I was opposed, in principle, to censorship. That seemed to prove conclusively that my function would be that of a "mouthpiece" defending guilty clients.

For all I know, the idea of retaining a "mouthpiece," who would be something of a lobbyist, may have entered the minds of some of the motion picture men. They were sincere, but they were bewildered. Some producers genuinely desired to clean house but did not know how. Trade practices of the period were chaotic and savagely competitive. There were charges and countercharges of stealing and of cutthroat methods.

Ironically, many exhibitors also attacked me and the offer that the producers and distributors had made — on diametrically opposite grounds. In me they seemed to see a threat of blue-nosed regulation and political pressure.

Of course I had no intention of being a lobbyist, mouthpiece, or fixer. The cry of the children who idolized the movie stars was now the "Macedonian Call" as far as I was concerned, and I was not going to betray them by becoming a political front-runner for a contaminated product.

But I knew I was still opposed to censorship.

The processes of democracy are long and slow and often discouraging. But I have always believed that the principle of self-regulation, as contrasted with regulation from without, will take firm root if given a chance; that, if watered by patience and optimism (a patience that seems weakness to reformers, and an optimism beyond discernible reason), the principle will at length flourish and prove lasting. This is because *self-regulation educates and strengthens those who practice it.*

And I have always felt that in a democratic commonwealth each business, each industry, and each art has as much right to, and as much duty toward, self-regulation as has the general citizenry to self-government. This, I understand, was the fundamental idea behind the medieval trade guilds — the ancestors of our professional associations as well as of our labor unions.

Now the motion picture men had proposed an Association. That was their own idea, and they were kind enough to ask me to be the head of it. All these considerations made me determine that my office would not be a mere control tower, nor would I be a "czar," but that our Association would function *democratically.*

However, acting as missionary for the democratic concept of "home rule" and self-regulation was only half my job, as I envisioned it. The other half was to educate the movie-going public.

Right here someone is going to ask the question: "If the producers were not giving the public what it wanted, how could they stay in business?"

The answer to that is twofold: first, they were in some danger of not remaining in business, and not merely because of reform leagues and angry legislators. Gross receipts, so large during World War I and in the early post-war period, had begun to decline. At the time I became spokesman only one banker, Otto H. Kahn, would do business with the industry at all. This one exception may be explained by Mr. Kahn's well-known benevolence toward anything artistic or even potentially artistic. He had endowed the Metropolitan Opera Company of New York, had built the Century Theater, and later, although not a Catholic, had become the philanthropic mainstay of the Catholic Writers' Guild.

The second part of the answer is that it cannot be moral or licit to supply an immoral or illicit demand. This is readily apparent in the case of the bootlegger, the smuggler, the narcotic peddler, and the pander. None of these things is legitimate. The motion picture industry was legitimate per se, and potentially a great force for good.

But self-regulation alone would not be enough. To make it worth while, *a demand had to be created for finer films*. There were cooperative services, too, which I felt the motion picture medium had an obligation to perform.

It was therefore my idea not only to try to compose the differences among the producing and distributing companies but also to urge the public, through women's clubs and various fine and influential groups, to encourage our growth — not with brickbats but with counsel and cooperation.

I knew it would not be easy, but I knew it could be done.

On January 14, 1922, I met with the producers in New York and gave them my answer.

In the days between my acceptance of the motion picture offer and the opening of the new office, it was interesting to watch the reactions — both in the press and in myself.

On the lighter side was a humorous cartoon of which the artist, Albert T. Reid, sent me an autographed print. It was titled "The Cynosure of Boyville," Two little urchins behind my back were discussing the reported salary when one broke in with, "Man! That ain't half of it. He gits to see all the movie shows for nothin'!" But in front of me, clasping my hand, another youngster is saying with a smile, "Gee, Mr. Hays — I congratulate you. I'd rather have your job than any job in the world."

That's about the way I felt myself.

Many people, however, either saw the industry as a frightful mess or thought I was going to march in like a dictator. But I remembered plenty of experiences in politics and in the Post Office Department which had proved that folks are willing and able to work together for a good end, if they can see it. I was sure that there were appeals in the movies capable of uniting industry and public in a joint program for better motion pictures.

That joint program was the keynote of my subsequent quarter century of effort. It never changed.

Of the industry leaders who were founding the Association, I said in my first press release of January 18, "I believe in the earnestness and integrity of their determination to carry out these purposes and am convinced of the possibilities of very large plans and successful consummation."

The statement of the founders' committee, professing similar faith in me, prophesied that the industry would move forward "to its predestined place of importance in the civilization of today and tomorrow." And I want to record, with gratitude and deep appreciation, that this "honeymoon" of January 1922 continued. As in all healthy human relations, there were often completely divergent points of view, once or twice so violently opposed that I broke the glass and cut my hand banging on the conference-table top. In so bitterly competitive an industry, it was often a struggle to find common ground, but in the end we usually got together and went ahead. Few men have been given a finer post-graduate course in the theory and practice of compromise, though I prefer to call it harmonization.

Sooner or later many appellations were bestowed on me. They included "Flm-Master," "Movie-Man," "Landis of the Films," "Family Doctor of the Movies," "The Cat's Whiskers," "Film Coordinator," "Hoosier Crusader," "Doctor of Celluloid," "The Little White Father of the Cinema." In the year following, "Czar" was most often used. And that reminds me of Governor Milliken's observation that this common use may have been partly due to the fact that a single column of type has room for only four letters of the largest size used. If so, this was an unfortunate trick of fate, for if there was anything that I was *not*, as executive of the new and voluntary association, it was a "czar."

One reference to a trade-paper opinion may help to round out the picture. The *Exhibitors' Herald* of March 18 carried in its announcement the subtitle, "Former Cabinet Member Announces Purposes and Aims during First Day as President of New Producer-Distributor Alliance." The mere statement must have sounded a bit brash! They reported me correctly when they quoted: "I want to make it clear that I do not come into this industry to crusade or do any of the radical things that have been pointed out as part of my work. I realize that I am entering a gigantic field of which I know little. My sole work for some time will be to acquaint myself with affairs so that I can best aid the men with whom I am associated to do jointly those things they are mutually, but not competitively, interested in doing. It is a tremendous undertaking and I approach it with much concern, but with that confidence which springs from an earnest purpose, and with the conviction that we will have the generous help of everyone in accomplishing what must be recognized as an effort for the good of all."

When I said that "my sole work for some time" would be to acquaint myself with affairs, I hadn't met the affairs! When I did meet them they were not disposed to wait for me to conclude any deliberate, academic study. They were already lying there on my desk, marked "urgent." So, in the reverse slogan of one of our military services, it was a question of "learn while you earn."

Although I couldn't have known it when I entered the new office on Monday morning, March 6, 1922, there was what modern executives would call a "ten-point program" waiting for attention. At least the first five of them could be dignified by the now familiar term "emergency." They were:

> *Internal Disorders*, such as bad trade practices and scandals
> *Censorship* and other threatened restrictions
> *Mexican Diplomatic Crisis* over American films
> Building a "more perfect *union*" in the industry, and one that would be self-governing
> Improving the *Quality* of pictures quickly
> Improving the *Demand*, through organized public opinion
> Securing the *Practical Cooperation of Educators*
> Helping *Distributors* to overcome fraud and loss
> Helping *Exhibitors* adjust contract problems
> Improving the quality of *Advertising*

Although this listing of exactly ten major items is of course an oversimplification, it is close to the facts. From my brief summary of the ten subjects hereafter, each can be seen to have been a project that couldn't wait. And though most of the problems were continuous, the initial approach to them was most important. In nearly every case circumstances forced me to take the bull by the horns and do something at once. It was far better to attack than to defend. ...

My first contract with the Association, dated April 15, 1922, was for three years. It was supplemented by a network of contracts by which the member companies bound themselves jointly and severally to guarantee the performance of the agreement. Even though there were times during that first year when some directors' meetings might have sounded through the keyhole like a street fight, we knew we were in this thing together, and we were going to see it through. In more than a quarter of a century I was never without a binding contract. And I never lost my belief that both the industry and the public would find, in better pictures, their common advantage.

The factors involved in the MPPDA relationships were carefully examined by Dr. Moley in preparation for his book, *The Hays Office*, the most thorough objective analysis yet made. At one point he says:

> Hays was not being chosen as "Czar" of the Industry. But neither was he being employed merely to ward off the impending danger of Federal and State censorship legislation. There was an abundance of problems which the perturbed film men were finally willing to recognize as common — the protection of the interest of producers and distributors in foreign countries; the theft and piracy of films; the revenue, copyright and tariff laws affecting the Industry.

One very human aspect of the situation he puts thus:

> Another feature of those preliminary discussions was the distrust some of the movie men felt for one another. . . . Each individual would have hotly denied that the thought of pulling out of this ambitious venture could ever cross his mind. But each was reasonably certain that others in the group were quite capable of such conduct. The multiplication of contracts was the measure of this mutual distrust as much as it was the measure of the individual enthusiasm with which these men regarded Hays. Each had become genuinely convinced, for the moment at any rate, that Hays must be the captain of his own fate and master of his own soul in the three years that lay ahead. . . .

Arriving on the California Limited late on Sunday afternoon, July 23, our party left the train at Pasadena, to be greeted by Jesse L. Lasky, Joseph M. Schenck, and Abraham Lehr, and taken to Mr. Lasky's home at Hillside and LaBrea Avenue for tea. Afterward I was asked by an interviewer if I felt nervous as I alighted from the train to begin this new adventure. I replied that our party included my boyhood chum Max Puett, Jim Connery, Maurice McKenzie, Fred Beetson, and Joe O'Neill. I am sure that had I gotten stage fright these good friends would have seen me through. As it happened, however, I was far too engrossed in our problems and in the work that lay ahead of us. . . .

The week ended in a blaze of glory with a mammoth all-industry rally at the Hollywood Bowl. This great outdoor amphitheatre, built in the hills above Hollywood and now nationally famous, was at that time just a huge excavation with a temporary stage; the granite tiers had not yet been installed. I am told that on Saturday afternoon, at the time of the rally, there were fifty thousand people present, and from where I sat on the rostrum, I could see that the place was not only jammed to overflowing but that crowds had taken positions of vantage on the surrounding hillsides. It was gratifying, too, to see that a large block of seats — I think about four hundred — had been reserved for the postal workers of the Los Angeles area.

The committee on arrangements included William S. Hart, chairman, Irving Thalberg, Mike Levee, B.F. Rosenberg, Glenn Harper, Jesse Lasky, Frank Woods, Sol Lesser, Bert Lytell, Joseph W. Engel, and John McCormick. Thanks to these gentlemen, everything went like clockwork. All the studios shut down at noon, and the personnel of each marched in a body to the great Bowl, many of the players in the costumes of the productions they were currently making. It was a riot of color, yet it all blended into a harmonious pattern on that glorious, cloudless summer day.

The gates of the Bowl were thrown open at half-past two, although in obedience to the decree of the committee I did not arrive until later. At the appointed hour I was escorted from Max Puett's home by a police detail, which preceded my car. At Hollywood Boulevard and Cahuenga Pass I joined the "big shots" and, as we turned off the boulevard to Highland Avenue, the American Legion band met us and marched ahead of us to the Bowl. Crowds lined the sidewalks, and everywhere I looked cameras were clicking. . . .

Hitherto I had spoken to individuals or to selected groups. I had spoken to the companies actually shooting on the days I had happened to visit the studios. Even at the banquet, the preceding Wednesday night, I had spoken mainly to the "elite." This time I had before me the entire fellowship of the "university," practically the whole population of filmdom.

Jesse Lasky was chairman of the historic occasion. I was introduced, however, by Dr. Allen Shore, president of the Hollywood (not Los Angeles) Chamber of Commerce, for this was Hollywood's day.

It was my day too. Tears came to my eyes as, spontaneously, the people of Hollywood rose and cheered. And while it took another ten years to evolve the Production Code which is now practically constitutional in the industry, the wedge had been driven. It was the first step to be judged not by its length but by the direction it took. The folks of Hollywood had bought the goods. . . .

Improving the Demand

Even as early as July of 1922, when I first visited Hollywood, my plea for a public demand for better movies was already backed by millions of Americans who had authorized me to present their requests. I had discussed the whole problem before the convention of the General Federation of Women's Clubs and the National

Education Association, and with the representatives of more than eighty civic, welfare, and religious organizations in a conference held in New York. Figuratively, I carried their proxies in my pocket. The organized development of public relations sentiment, via an active committee, consumed a good deal of my time for the next few years.

I considered the movies to be an activity which should be judged in the light of its total impact on great numbers of people. It should be responsive to public demand, and although the Association was organized and financed by motion picture companies to promote their common interests and interpret those to the public, I personally felt an equal obligation to interpret the wishes of the public to the industry. I saw my task, again, as one of *mediation*, and I took my stand on the threshold of a two-way "open door." At once we set out to make our customers our friends and advisers. Booster and knocker must alike be heard. As to the most violent critics, I recalled my father's advice to "get so close to the mule he can't kick you"; and the well-wishers must be shown ways to make their good will bring practical results. I question whether any other industry has ever made such a record of organizing active good will in its support on so large a scale. So great became the volunteer force of cooperators, affiliated with the industry through our Public Relations Department, that as many as 600,000 men and women at one time were doing something on an organized basis for better pictures. And we made it an affirmative force: "What kind of pictures do you want?" was calculated to do producers more good than "What kind do you not want?" Here was a chance — indeed, a necessity — for a public relations job on a really grand scale. . . .

Incidentally, there was one thing I had to be careful about. Because widely advertised as a Presbyterian elder and incorrectly called a czar, I sometimes bent over backward to erase any impression of being a "bluenose" censor. I didn't mind a prominent cartoon of me in the latter role, but I didn't want it taken seriously. In Hollywood I saw to it that I danced with some of the stars and attended many of the social events. Since I've always enjoyed dancing, this part of my job was not difficult.

Before leaving this period I want to mention briefly some matters handled by various departments of the Association as early steps in our program.

In the field of public relations and information, I sought frequent occasion to "report to the public, " as in effect their representative. Close relations were maintained with the press, and our Speakers' Bureau kept busy. Activity in foreign countries was steadily promoted as it was increasingly realized that pictures constitute a universal language. Exhibitors and distributors were aided by the introduction of a standard exhibition contract, with its arbitration clause. Only 17 cases out of 5,450 in the first year were taken to the courts after an arbitration board had made its award. In the field of conservation, better protection against both fire and theft was developed. Better copyright legislation and title registration saved money and headaches, and helped to kill the "sex film title." Similar progress was made in preventing "salacious, misleading, and dishonest advertising."

In progress toward a production code, ninety-one stories in a year were barred from the movies, and twenty-four companies were using the new MPPDA emblem. We measurably prevented the then prevalent types of books and plays from invading our pictures.

With the cooperation of editors, tremendous sentiment was marshaled against censorship. Aid was given in cases where unreasonable admission taxes had been slapped on. Connecticut was the best example. Here, in 1925, a tax of twenty dollars per reel was levied on every reel brought into the state. With the cooperation of distributors and exhibitors, a method of splitting and taking care of the tax was worked out, until the law was repealed the next year. . . .

MOLLY HASKELL
The Twenties

Extracts from the chapter on the 1920s in From Reverence to Rape: The Treatment of Women in the Movies *(Holt, Rinehart & Winston, 1974). Here are some examples of this critic's brilliant ability to provide telling and descriptive phrases, revealing the "images" presented by certain stars in the silent era. Read this a few times and note how first-rate humanist criticism can illuminate our social and psychological understanding of movies.*

In the ferment over women's rights and the loosening of the cultural stays, the twenties seem closer to our time than any intervening decade. They seem, indeed, the antecedent to the current women's liberation movement and the "new morality" and, more, to anticipate the split between the two. Just as the serious and political "Apollonian" side of the current women's movement seems often opposed to the hedonistic and sexual "Dionysian" side, so the "emancipated woman" of the twenties was either a suffragette or a flapper, depending on what she wanted and how she chose to get it. In an interview not too long ago, Anita Loos, scoffing at the tactics of today's feminists, said that women always knew they were more intelligent than men, but that in the twenties they were smart enough not to let men know it. But it is precisely this kind of duplicity, the holy fallacy of women's inferiority that current feminists — and yesteryear's suffragettes — challenge. For the Anita Loos' flapper, who wanted social and sexual, rather than political and intellectual, power, this was a gold-plated philosophy. As long as she played dumb she could stay on her pedestal. But the suffragette (who rarely made her way into films) was more honest. She wanted direct, not indirect, power and authority, and her approach was uningratiatingly direct.

Women won suffrage in 1920 and were admitted to the nominating conventions of both major parties the same year. Even before suffrage, women had begun to enter the professions and, as the decade dawned, more were choosing to do so. By the twenties, plays and novels were increasingly focusing on the "new woman," some to encourage her, others to satirize her. But it was awhile before such a rebel, even in flapper form, penetrated film. Decades are artificial divisions, full of contradictions, particularly in film where there is always a partial lag. The spirit of anarchy and experimentation we associate with the twenties, with Fitzgerald and Stein and Hemingway and Paris and Freud and German Expressionism did not filter into film until a much later date. It was really in the early thirties that the revolutionary twenties' spirit, at least the questioning of marriage and conventional morality, took hold. But in the twenties, DeMille and even von Stroheim introduced intrigue and sexual excitement to marital drama without really challenging the basic sense and sanctity of the institution. For the most part, Victorian values prevailed in silent films and even as the "It" girl came sashaying into view, the rural sweetheart, for which Mary Pickford was the prototype, continued to claim the loyalty of a huge number of Americans. And even the "It" girl, who, with her inventor, the British novelist Elinor Glyn, became a naturalized Hollywood citizen, was not as naughty as she seemed, but rather a disturber of the peace redeemable by marriage.

There was nevertheless a dialectic between the "new" and the "old-fashioned woman" (a power struggle that D.W. Griffith obviously felt when he began "modernizing" his heroines) that was reflected in the corresponding opposition between the city and the country as the real heart of America. The country was the repository of traditional values that, for Griffith and F.W. Murnau, Pickford and Gish, were pure, noble, and true; but for DeMille, or Lubitsch, or Clara Bow, these same values were narrow, repressive, and old hat. For both groups the sense of strong contrasts and extremes that was aesthetically crucial to silent film became morally determining. Lacking speech, movies had to tell their stories through image and incident, and through characters with an instantly identifiable iconography. The morality play names — "the Man," "the Wife," "the Woman from the City" — used by Murnau in Sunrise are indicative of the allegorical nature of silent film generally. (As a sidelight, it's worth noting the double standard unconsciously expressed in the labels "the Man" and "the Wife," the male being defined by gender only, the female by her marital status.)

In the identification of physical type with role, the films of Murnau and his colleagues bear a close resemblance to the "typage" method of Eisenstein — a director who in other ways was Murnau's antithesis. Developed from the Russian director's interest in Oriental drama and calligraphy, "typage" dictated that an actor be cast according to his physical resemblance to a part, to the "idea" of a workingman or an aristocrat. The American categories corresponding to Eisenstein's types differ less in kind than in shadings, being moral rather than political, implicitly, rather than explicitly, didactic. But such instantly recognizable types as the "virgin" (fair-haired and tiny), the "vamp" (dark and sultry, larger than the "virgin," but smaller than the "mother") and the "woman of the world" (a sophisticated blend of the "virgin's" soul and the "vamp's" facade) are as stylized within an American context as the ritualistic figures of Kabuki and Noh drama. . . .

From the twenties' frizzy-haired flapper to the seventies' long-haired model, we are never quite as unique as we think we are. If the stars of the twenties look, to our unfamiliar eyes, like an old group photograph in which the distinguishing traits have disappeared and only the physical similarities remain, we too — and the stars who represent us — may look astonishingly alike to our grandchildren. It is one of the properties of perspective that from a distance of time, or space, everyone, like the Chinese, looks alike.

If the women stars of the twenties were more defined by type than the men — as women always are — they were also more colorful and more central to the myths of the period. The action heroes and the male comedians had a world to themselves, but most of the films of the twenties (a larger proportion than in other decades) were romances and melodramas dominated by a single star, billed above the title, and the women stars outnumbered their male counterparts. Different types coexisted. These were genuinely wild, experimental days in Hollywood, before sound, before the Crash, and before the social crusaders came in, in the form of the Legion of Decency in the early thirties, to legislate morals and arbitrate between good and evil in films. Stars were demoted by box-office failure rather than by social pressure. The falling star of Theda Bara, who reached the peak of her vampire's powers (and largely publicity-induced popularity) in 1915, met Mary Pickford's star going the other way the same year that Griffith's *Birth of a Nation* introduced Lillian Gish. Gish, in turn, would be succeeded by a long line of replica mirror-image virgins.

At this juncture of the Victorian moral world and the allegorical tendency of silent film, the virgin emerges in her purest form, fair-haired, delicate, and above all: tiny, in the time-honored tradition of the "weaker sex." (The symbolic importance of size suggests that women's increased height over the years has influenced their changing self-image.) But it is a true innocence — as if she, like the industry, like the country, had not yet been deflowered — an innocence that belongs not just to her, but to the way she is seen, to the eye of her beholder. For, in the nineteenth-century imagination of such directors as Griffith and Borzage, the vision of woman idealized and debased, above and below, was, as George Eliot suggested in *The Mill on the Floss*, metaphysically the same. By the romantic code, woman's chastity was a correlative of male honor, her Fall, of his concupiscence and guilt. The notion of the virgin ideal unfortunately outlived the romantic code which gave it plausibility. In film, subsequent virgins, like the medium itself, would be tainted by self-consciousness at best, at worst, depicted in venom, the underside of a chivalry gone sour and of sexual uncertainty in a world of fluctuating values.

But throughout the twenties, the virgin-heroine was still rooted in the romantic spirit of mutual reverence. As late as 1927 and 1928, in Janet Gaynor's sublimely sentimental heroines of *Seventh Heaven* and *Street Angel*, she is alive and well, her chastity imperiled but her purity intact.

Such glistening icons of femininity as Gaynor and Gish were often steely underneath but they belonged to the "women-rule-the-world-but-don't-tell-anybody" school and they made a point of concealing their strength. (We can be sure that when Gish directed her own film she gave orders — or made requests — like a lady, never raising her voice above a genteel chirp.)

The image of Gaynor as one of the most ethereal of the angel-heroines comes primarily from the two Borzage films, *Seventh Heaven* and *Street Angel*. As an expression of Borzage's Italian-Catholic romantic sensibility, she is a kind of Madonna of the streets, an urban peasant sanctified by a vocation for love and sacrifice. She is the perfect example of the woman who, in the metaphysical, religious vision of Borzage, combines the virgin and the whore, as in *Street Angel* she literally, but only temporarily, takes to the streets. (In an exception that proves the rule, a Raoul Walsh thirties' movie called *The Man Who Came Back*, she would play a fallen woman to no avail.)

It is interesting to compare the way Borzage uses, and exalts, her with the way Murnau treats her in *Sunrise*. Just as she is paired with the towering Charles Farrell in *Seventh Heaven* and *Street Angel* to emphasize both her vulnerability and the miracle of her inner strength, she is paired in *Sunrise* with the enormous George O'Brien. But the emphasis here is on O'Brien's character — the Frankenste-inish horror of a man possessed by the devil. The film focuses on his moral dilemma, and Gaynor, her hair pulled back in a severe bun, merges with the animals, the rustic simplicity of the home, the country, to become a symbol of the "good." She is a part of nature for Murnau, an element in a directorial style that in subordinating the actress to the overall vision, distinguishes the "art film" from the "star vehicle." As Borzage worships her like a Madonna, he treats her like a star. Framed in a halo of backlighting and soft focus, her eyes raised romantically and religiously to her man-god, she galvanizes attention in an ecstasy of feeling, a submissiveness that assures her of preeminence.

In both *Seventh Heaven*, where she agonizes in her garret flat for the return of her soldier-lover, and *Street Angel*, where she is a poverty-stricken Cinderella who sacrifices herself to save her artist-husband, she is seen as plain and ordinary and yet transfigured by love. Where there is something naturally refined and aristocratic about Gish, Gaynor represents the common people, the peasant turned saint. She is round-faced, fluffy-haired, mincing, a "good girl," who by doing a supreme right is transfigured into a goddess; an ordinary actress who, through Borzage's direction, through a counterpointing of doll-like gestures and enormous, radiant close-ups, achieves an incredible emotional intensity. . . .

Lillian Gish, the least modern of Griffith's heroines, is in many ways the most emotionally resourceful and intense. She is flower-like and naive, delicate as a figurine but durable as an ox, and her fascination arises from a contradiction between the two, between her daintiness and the ferocity with which she maintains it. Her movements — her agitated gestures and flutteriness — can be more erotic than the explicit semaphore of the vamp, since they suggest the energy of pent-up sexuality engaged in its own suppression. And yet she is more often tragic than gay. As the miserable waif of *Broken Blossoms*, she must use her hands to force her lips into a smile. The images in *Way Down East* of a young mother cradling her dead baby in her arms and later seeking destruction on the ice-covered river are as primal as anything in our film consciousness; they are expressions of a life-and-death force that is both greater than man or womankind, yet altogether female.

Mae Marsh is already several degrees more sophisticated, more "grown up," more urban. She looks at the world with a candor and sense of humor lacking in the sublimely chaste Gish. She is closer to being a "working woman" and is the halfway heroine between Gish and Carol Dempster, the leading lady of Griffith's later films, done at a time when the vestal virgin was in box-office decline and he had to make his bid to keep up with the fashions.

Dempster, more modern and self-sufficient than Gish, is a heroine most people feel more comfortable with today. She is the driving force that keeps a poverty-stricken family alive in *Isn't Life Wonderful?* In *Sorrows of Satan*, she is actually an authoress, living in rags in a garret and writing away by candlelight. And yet, it is not always the "working" women who have, simply by definition, the greatest character and sense of self. Dempster is a working girl, but her vivacity and initiative seem willed into being — probably because Griffith himself isn't convinced. Gish's old-fashioned resilience, on the other hand, springs from a character more subtle and rounded, more complete within herself. . . .

While Gish's agitation has sexual roots, Pickford's is an affectation of childish ebullience and masks a calculating spirit. As the little hands clap in glee, the little mind is contriving how to get what it wants, how to charm the little boy or the disagreeable old man. The fact that she came to these child roles late in her career, in her maturity, only confirms that unwillingness to grow up she shares with a huge portion of the American public, who flocked to these pictures in an orgy of misty-eyed infantilism.

The urge to return to childhood, to recover an innocence both historical and personal, is as deeply ingrained in the American psyche as the idealism that, corrupted, gives rise to it. It is the escape valve from the responsibilities and disillusionments — particularly the disillusionments — of marriage and family, of growing up and old. From dreary adult realities, a woman reverts to childhood, the spoiled state of daughterhood, or even to adolescence, when everything was still possible and ideal, not yet delimited by sexual or domestic submission. A man may travel back down the dusty road to childhood through the Huck Finn adventurer or Skippy and Sooky or the Dead End kids, but childhood contains bitter memories of helplessness and dependency. He is more likely to seek his El Dorado by escaping to a world of action or of comic defiance, that is, a world without, or subversive of, women.

The flight from women and the fight against them in their role as entrappers and civilizers is one of the major underlying themes of American cinema: it is the impetus behind such genres as the Western and the silent comedy. The comic spirit, particularly in the rambunctious, anarchic forms of silent comedy, or the debunking shafts of verbal wit, is basically masculine in gender and often antifeminine in intention. . . .

The titles of the films suggest more succinctly than any plot synopsis could that marvelous, contradictory blend of Victorian prudery, Dickensian melodrama, and the "new morality" that were the ingredients of the jazz film: *The Careless Woman, The Little Snob, Foolish Wives, Strictly Unconventional, The Lure of the Night Club, Wickedness Preferred, Speed Crazed, The Good-Bad Wife, Souls for Sables, Lady of the Pavements, Madonna of the Streets, Rose of the Tenements, Why Change Your Wife?,* and *Why Bring That Up?.* These were not lyrical love stories or mere escapist fantasies, but lurid melodramas in which infidelity, illegitimacy, blackmail, suicide, larceny, and murder figured, not only in the same film, but often within minutes of each other. The material came mostly from magazine stories and popular stage plays and ranged indiscriminately from high style to low life, from international intrigues to backwater scandal, covering the glories and penalties of both.

As often as not women were the authors and adapters of these screenplays and thus helped fashion the image of the flapper and woman of the world, but it was the actresses who gave them their final, quite different forms. Anita Loos' flapper is different from Elinor Glyn's, but the difference between Clara Bow and Norma Talmadge is the more striking. Bow, the "It" girl, was urban and lower, or lower-middle, class; Talmadge, even when she played working girls, suggested a more privileged, upper-middle-class background. But both brought these backgrounds (with their suggestion of family and moral pressure, and, ultimately, puritanism) with them, whereas Joan Crawford and Gloria Swanson, self-invented "stars" in the truest sense, came out of nowhere and were freer to follow the inclinations of the moment. The burden of conscience, and social context, that kept the flapper from going too far didn't cast its shadow of guilt over Swanson and Crawford; thus they enjoyed a freedom that is closer to the European *femme fatale*.

But generally the American flapper was, by definition, only superficially uninhibited. She was, after all, the middle-class (whether upper or lower) daughter of puritans, and she would pass this heritage on to her own daughters and granddaughters. As the flaming incarnation of the flapper spirit, Clara Bow suggests sensuality and wildness but doesn't stray any farther from the straight and narrow than the distance of a long cigarette holder or a midnight joy ride. She is the twentieth century pitted against the nineteenth, urban against rural society, the liberated working girl against the Victorian valentine, the boisterous flapper against Lillian Gish's whispering wild flower. But Clara Bow's recklessness is as deceptive as Lillian Gish's delicacy. In Victor Seastrom's *The Wind*, Gish is buffeted, literally, by more ill winds than Clara Bow will ever know. At her wickedest, Bow might flirt with a married man, but he would usually be superseded by an appropriate suitor in a relationship sanctified by marriage. Even her sensuality, the soft contours and roundness of her body, were babyish, schoolgirlish — a quality Dorothy Arzner caught in *The Wild Party*. An early sound film, this story of a college girl in love with her professor (Fredric March), is unremarkable except for the very sensual handling of Clara Bow and her pals in the girls' dormitory and for Bow's "male" code of loyalty and camaraderie. Her image — formed, really, by

Elinor Glyn, who wrote *It* and *Three Week Ends* — is that of an innocent sybarite, and her films, like her morals, are more good-humored than heavy-breathing. . . .

In many ways, the vessels of purity played by Lillian Gish and Mae Marsh, Griffith's rearguard heroines, experienced more sexual mishap and took more sexual abuse (always of course rebounding in the end) than those brazen shockers, the flapper and the party girl. It is the sexual chastity of Bow rather than of Gish that we understand today, because it is hidden beneath the bravado of a woman of the world. It is the bravado, moreover, of a woman afraid of losing control, and there is not much difference between Clara Bow, who does it with no one, and the character Jane Fonda plays in *Klute*, who does it with everyone; both are women going about the business of saving their fragile egos and both are in danger of losing their souls.

While Americans responded to the alien exoticism of types like Theda Bara, Swanson, and Negri, Europeans grooved on the perverse innocence of Clara Bow. The attraction of opposites (the *esprit de contradiction*) and the dialectic between the American and the European woman has operated as both the theme and the source of underlying tension in films from the twenties to the seventies. A two-part dialectic, it is the conflict between the European woman's ease with her body and her relative enslavement to traditional social values and the American woman's anxiety over her body and relative social freedom.

An instinct for contrast, and the compensation factor, figure almost automatically in the work of directors who, like critics, find their erotic fancies tickled by women who are at opposite sides of the sexual-cultural pole from themselves. Thus for Josef von Sternberg, a launderer from Brooklyn with an acquired Viennese sensibility, Marlene Dietrich, a woman redolent of the demimonde and smoke-filled cabarets, became the vessel of his obsessions, while German director G.W. Pabst, in his search for the ideal Lulu for *Pandora's Box*, found Dietrich, his countrywoman, too "old" and too "knowing." Instead, and against the advice of those around him (and to the everlasting resentment of his compatriots), he opted for the gleaming unworldliness of Louise Brooks, a relatively unknown American actress. She had appeared, not greatly to her advantage, in Howard Hawks' *A Girl in Every Port*, where she was the third wheel in a male friendship. In *Love 'Em and Leave "Em* she was charmingly uninhibited, but in the secondary role of Evelyn Brent's bad sister. It remained for Pabst to make her a star, exposing her animal sensuality and turning her into one of the most erotic figures on the screen — the bold, black-helmeted young girl who, with only a shy grin to acknowledge her "fall," becomes a prostitute in *Diary of a Lost Girl* and who, with no more sense of sin than a baby, drives men out of their minds in *Pandora's Box*.

One difference between the sophisticated comedies and melodramas of DeMille and those of Europeans like Stroheim, Lubitsch and Sternberg, was that DeMille allotted his women less space — architectural and emotional — for the development and analysis of feelings. These expatriates in America automatically brought with them a sense of contrast, brought real wit and style to Hollywood, and, in the back lots of Paramount and Universal and M-G-M, created an imaginary continent of romantic intrigue, of innocents abroad and philandering royalty, translating their own obsessions into those of their characters.

ROBERT S. LYND AND
HELEN MERRELL LYND
Inventions Remaking Leisure

From pages 263-268 of Middletown: A Study in American
Culture *(Harcourt Brace, 1929). These thoughtful and hardwork-
ing social scientists, in a famous book, indicated in just six pages
what should have been done down through the years in film study.
They asked what was going on in a typical town, what movies the
people went to, what the movies appeared to be saying to them, and
what stars they loved. The lost chances in social science and film research are apparent here and they continue to be lost. Further questioning could have revealed what particular climaxes and scenes
meant to viewers and how the power of "the pictures" met and enlarged their attitudes and passions.*

Like the automobile, the motion picture is more to Middletown
than simply a new way of doing an old thing; it has added new
dimensions to the city's leisure. To be sure, the spectacle-watching
habit was strong upon Middletown in the nineties. Whenever they
had a chance people turned out to a "show," but chances were
relatively fewer. Fourteen times during January, 1890, for instance,
the Opera House was opened for performances ranging from Uncle
Tom's Cabin to The Black Crook, before the paper announced that
"there will not be any more attractions at the Opera House for nearly
two weeks." In July there were no "attractions"; a half dozen were
scattered through August and September; there were twelve in
October.

Today nine motion picture theaters operate from 1 to 11 p.m.
seven days a week summer and winter; four of the nine give three
different programs a week, the other five having two a week; thus
twenty-two different programs with a total of over 300 performances are available to Middletown every week in the year. In
addition, during January, 1923, there were three plays in Middletown and four motion pictures in other places than the regular
theaters, in July three plays and one additional movie, in October
two plays and one movie.

About two and three-fourths times the city's entire population
attended the nine motion picture theaters during the month of July,
1923, the "valley" month of the year, and four and one-half times
the total population in the "peak" month of December. Of 395 boys
and 457 girls in the three upper years of the high school who stated
how many times they had attended the movies in "the last seven

days," a characteristic week in mid-November, 30 percent of the boys and 39 percent of the girls had not attended, 31 and 29 percent respectively had been only once, 22 and 21 percent, respectively two times, 10 and 7 percent, three times, and 7 and 4 percent, four or more times. According to the housewives interviewed regarding the custom in their own families, in three of the forty business class families interviewed and in thirty-eight of the 122 working class families no member "goes at all" to the movies. One family in ten in each group goes as an entire family once a week or oftener; the two parents go together without their children once a week or oftener in four business class families (one in ten), and in two working class families (one in sixty); in fifteen business class families and in thirty-eight working class families the children were said by their mothers to go without their parents one or more times weekly.

In short, the frequency of movie attendance of high school boys and girls is about equal, business class families tend to go more often than do working class families, and children of both groups attend more often without their parents than do all the individuals or other combinations of family members put together. The decentralizing tendency of the movies upon the family, suggested by this last, is further indicated by the fact that only 21 percent of 337 boys and 33 percent of 423 girls in the three upper years of the high school go to the movies more often with their parents than without them. On the other hand, the comment is frequently heard in Middletown that movies have cut into lodge attendance, and it is probable that time formerly spent in lodges, saloons, and unions is now being spent in part at the movies, at least occasionally with other members of the family. Like the automobile and radio, the movies, by breaking up leisure time into an individual, family, or small group affair, represent a counter movement to the trend toward organization so marked in clubs and other leisure-time pursuits.

How is life being quickened by the movies for the youngsters who bulk so large in the audiences, for the punch press operator at the end of his working day, for the wife who goes to a "picture" every week or so "while he stays home with the children," for those business class families who habitually attend?

"Go to a motion picture . . . and let yourself go," Middletown reads in a *Saturday Evening Post* advertisement. "Before you know it you are *living* the story — laughing, loving, hating, struggling, winning! All the adventure, all the romance, all the excitement you lack in your daily life are in —— Pictures. They take you completely out of yourself into a wonderful new world. . . . Out of the cage of every-day existence! If only for an afternoon or an evening — escape!

The program of the five cheaper houses is usually a "Wild West" feature, and a comedy; of the four better houses, one feature film, usually a "society" film but frequently Wild West or comedy, one short comedy, or if the feature is a comedy, an educational film (e.g., *Laying an Ocean Cable* or *Making a Telephone*), and a news film. In general, people do not go to the movies to be instructed; the Yale Press series of historical films, as noted earlier, were a flat failure and the local exhibitor discontinued them after the second picture. As in the case of the books it reads, comedy, heart interest, and adventure compose the great bulk of what Middletown enjoys in the movies. Its heroes, according to the manager of the leading theater, are, in the order named, Harold Lloyd, comedian; Gloria Swanson, heroine in modern society films; Thomas Meighan, hero in modern society films; Colleen Moore, ingénue; Douglas Fairbanks, comedian and adventurer; Mary Pickford, ingénue; and Norma Talmadge, heroine in modern society films. Harold Lloyd comedies draw the largest crowds. "Middletown is amusement hungry," says the opening sentence in a local editorial; at the comedies Middletown lives for an hour in a happy sophisticated make-believe world that leaves it, according to the advertisement of one film, "happily convinced that Life is very well worth living."

Next largest are the crowds which come to see the sensational society films. The kind of vicarious living brought to Middletown by these films may be inferred from such titles as: "*Alimony* — brilliant men, beautiful jazz babies, champagne baths, midnight revels, petting parties in the purple dawn, all ending in one terrific smashing climax that makes you gasp"; "*Married Flirts — Househusbands:* Do you flirt? Does your wife always know where you are? Are you faithful to your vows? *Wives:* What's your hubby doing? Do you know? Do you worry? Watch out for *Married Flirts.*" So fast do these flow across the silver screen that, e.g., at one time *The Daring Years, Sinners in Silk, Women Who Give,* and *The Price She Paid* were all running synchronously, and at another "*Name the Man* — a story of betrayed womanhood," *Rouged Lips,* and *The Queen of Sin.* While Western "action" films and a million-dollar spectacle like *The Covered Wagon* or *The Hunchback of Notre Dame* draw heavy houses, and while managers lament that there are too few of the popular comedy films, it is the film with burning "heart interest" that packs Middletown's motion picture houses week after week. Young Middletown enters eagerly into the vivid experience of *Flaming Youth*: "neckers, petters, white kisses, red kisses, pleasure-mad daughters, sensation-craving mothers, by an author who didn't dare sign his name; the truth bold, naked, sensational" — so ran the press advertisement —

under the spell of the powerful conditioning medium of pictures presented with music and all possible heightening of the emotional content, and the added factor of sharing this experience with a "date" in a darkened room. Meanwhile, *Down to the Sea in Ships*, a costly spectacle of whaling adventure, failed at the leading theater "because," the exhibitor explained, "the whale is really the hero in the film and there wasn't enough 'heart interest' for the women."

Actual changes of habits resulting from the week-after-week witnessing of these films can only be inferred. Young Middletown is finding discussion of problems of mating in this new agency that boasts in large illustrated advertisements, "Girls! You will learn how to handle 'em!" and "Is it true that marriage kills love? If you want to know what love really means, its exquisite torture, its overwhelming raptures, see ——."

"Sheiks and their 'shebas'," according to the press account of the Sunday opening of one film, " . . . sat without a movement or a whisper through the presentation. . . . It was a real exhibition of love-making and the youths and maidens of [Middletown] who thought that they knew something about the art found that they still had a great deal to learn."

Some high school teachers are convinced that the movies are a powerful factor in bringing about the "early sophistication" of the young and the relaxing of social taboos. One working class mother frankly welcomes the movies as an aid in child-rearing, saying, "I send my daughter because a girl has to learn the ways of the world somehow and the movies are a good safe way." The judge of the juvenile court lists the movies as one of the "big four" causes of local juvenile delinquency, believing that the disregard of group mores by the young is definitely related to the witnessing week after week of fictitious behavior sequences that habitually link the taking of long chances and the happy ending. While the community attempts to safeguard its schools from commercially intent private hands, this powerful new educational instrument, which has taken Middletown unawares, remains in the hands of a group of men — an ex-peanut-stand proprietor, an ex-bicycle racer and race promoter, and so on — whose primary concern is making money. . . .

Save for some efforts among certain of the women's clubs to "clean up the movies" and the opposition of the Ministerial Association to "Sunday movies," Middletown appears content in the main to take the movies at their face value — "a darned good show" — and largely disregard their educational or habit-forming aspects.

Chapter 3

Some Shining Examples

ROBERT E. MORSBERGER
Tol'able David

Review reprinted from Frank N. Magill, Magill's Survey of Cinema: *Silent Films (Salem Press, 1982).*

Released: 1921
Production: Charles Duell, Henry King, and Richard Barthelmess for Associated First National
Direction: Henry King
Screenplay: Edmund Goulding; based on a short story of the same name by Joseph Hergesheimier
Cinematography: Henry Cronjager
Length: 7 reels/7,118 feet

Principal characters:

David Kinemon	Richard Barthelmess
Esther Hatburn	Gladys Hulette
Luke Hatburn	Ernest Torrence
Allen Kinemon	Warner Richmond
Mrs. Kinemon, David's mother	Marion Abbott
Mr. Kinemon, David's father	Edmund Gurney
Rose Kinemon, Allen's wife	Patterson Dial
John Gault	Lawrence Eddinger

Director Henry King (1892 -   ) had one of the longest careers in film history, from a few minor films in 1916 to the 1962 production, *Tender Is the Night*. In the era of sound films, he became a director at Twentieth Century Fox, where he turned out innumerable Tyrone Power films and made many well-crafted pictures, such as *The Song of Bernadette* (1943). King's career was so long and he made so many films, a large number of which were routine commercial fare, that his reputation has not received all the credit it deserves. King has excelled at the vivid re-creation of old-fashioned and rural Americana in such films as *Stella Dallas* (1925), *The Winning of Barbara Worth* (1926), *State Fair* (1933), *Ramona* (1936), *Jesse James* (1939), *Margie* (1946), *The Gunfighter* (1950), *Wait 'Till the Sun Shines, Nellie* (1952), and *Carousel* (1956). The best regarded of King's pictures of Americana is the very first of the genre, *Tol'able David*, made in 1921.

Based on a short story by Joseph Hergesheimer, *Tol'able David* takes place during the horse-and-buggy era in the town of Greenfield, a tranquil West Virginia mountain community. The valley in which Greenfield lies is an idyllic place, both geographically and socially, for the town is a closely knit community in which people treat one another with respect and dignity. Young David Kinemon (Richard Barthelmess), however, is only "tol'able," for he is too small, too young, and too inexperienced to be given the respect due a proven man. David is an idealistic dreamer for whom the mountain and valley landscape is poetically beautiful. He is in love with Esther Hatburn (Gladys Hulette), who returns his affection.

The idyll is shattered by the arrival of three Hatburn cousins, degenerate criminals fleeing from the law in another state, who are relatives of Gladys and who take refuge at her father's farm, There, they terrorize the family and neighbors who cross their path. David is outraged at the way they order Esther and her father around, but she urges him to leave matters alone and not interfere lest the situation become even worse. When the brothers kill the Kinemons' dog Rocket for casual sport, however, David's older brother Allen (Warner Richmond) goes to challenge them. While Allen is denouncing their viciousness and threatening to go for the law, the oldest Hatburn brother, Luke (Ernest Torrence), strikes him from behind with a boulder and then steps savagely on his head. As a result, Allen is crippled for life. Only a few weeks earlier, the family had been celebrating the birth of a child to Allen and his wife Rose (Patterson Dial), but now Allen is a helpless invalid, and his wife is embittered.

Nevertheless, the sheriff is afraid to do anything, and the posse that had been pursuing the brothers cannot cross the state line. When Allen's and David's father (Edmund Gurney) takes down his rifle and prepares to fight the Hatburns, he is stricken with a fatal heart attack. David swears to avenge his father and brother, but his mother (Marion Abbot) begs him not to risk his own life too, and he reluctantly gives in to her pleas. With the father dead and Allen no longer able to keep his job as a driver of the mail, the family has to give up their farm and move into poor lodgings in town. David is now head of the family, but the townspeople consider him too young and untested to hold a position of responsibility.

He does get a job helping out in the store of John Gault (Lawrence Eddinger), the richest man in town. Gault is also the postmaster, and one day when the mail driver is too drunk to make his rounds, Gault entrusts the mail route to David. During the run, the Hatburn brothers waylay him and try to steal the mail. The monstrous brothers try to terrify David, but although he is small and little more than a boy, he defends himself, shoots two of the sadistic Hatburns, and has a desperate hand-to-hand fight with the oldest and most brutal brother. Although Hatburn is much larger and a vicious veteran of dirty fighting, David stands up to him. The fight is one of the most savage on film. David is shot and brutally beaten, but he desperately fights on and succeeds in killing Luke Hatburn. It has been a case of little David overcoming Goliath. Then, despite his injuries, David drives the mail back the rest of the route and returns to town. He collapses, but he has proven himself worthy of the trust given him and has shown the townspeople that he is considerably more than "tol'able."

A synopsis of the film sounds melodramatic, but *Tol'able David* transcends its plot, thanks largely to a sensitive performance by Richard Barthelmess and outstanding direction by King. King was from the Shenandoah Valley of Virginia, and instead of filming the picture on a Hollywood back lot, he went on location to the scenes of his boyhood and provided a remarkably authentic picture of rural American life and folkways in the homespun days. The screenplay is attributed to Edmund Goulding, an Englishman who later became a distinguished director himself with such films as *The Dawn Patrol* (1938), but Goulding was unfamiliar with the details of Appalachian life, and so King rewrote a good deal of the story, putting in considerable detail from his own early experience, such as having the family kneel around the chairs each night for prayers. Goulding was worried that King had ruined the story, but Hergesheimer was delighted and told the director, "You put into this all the things that I left out."

Instead of playing up the melodrama of the narrative, King gave the film a leisurely pace and dwelt lovingly on details of valley and village life, family and community relationships, and the Appalachian countryside and culture, all beautifully photographed in a way that provides a vivid record of a part of Americana that was already passing. The Russian film directors greatly admired *Tol'able David* for is *mise-en-scène* and use of montage, and Vsevolod Pudovkin discussed it at length as a superb example of the use of plastic cinematic material. The reviewer for *The New York Times* observed that the story follows the formula for homespun melodrama but that this time the dramá and the people seem real. "Tol'able David is sentimental in places, but not sloppy. It is bucolic, but its rusticity is not rubbed in."

The cast members were uniformly fine, with Barthelmess outdoing himself. A year before, he had played a similar role in D.W. Griffiths' *Way Down East*, as an honest farm boy who loves Lillian Gish, but in *Tol'able David*, he abandoned some annoying mannerisms, exaggerated stances, and a foolish yokelish grin. Instead, he imparted to David a combination of gentle sensitivity and grace under pressure that made him embody some of the best qualities of youthful idealism. Although he was twenty-six years old at the time, Barthelmess was entirely convincing as a teenage boy. He gave the finest performance of his career, and David is the role for which he is best remembered. Although he made five more films with King, none of them was nearly as good. With the coming of sound, Barthelmess' career declined (although his performance in the 1930 *The Dawn Patrol* is outstanding), and he retired from films in 1942.

In 1930, *Tol'able David* was remade as a sound film, directed by John G. Blystone, with Richard Cromwell in the title role, but this version lacks the authenticity of its predecessor and has fallen into well-deserved obscurity. The 1921 version remains one of the great silent films and the masterpiece of both Barthelmess and King.

TOM SHALES
Miss Lulu Bett

A review by Tom Shales in The American Film Heritage, published by the American Film Institute, printed in Washington, D.C. by Acropolis Books, 1972

[Almost everyone has heard of Cecil B. De Mille. He was hard to ignore. But for every Cecil we know, there's a William we don't know — in this case, Cecil's brother, whose work was largely ignored for forty years. Film preservation can help to correct such oversights, and the eight de Mille features acquired from Paramount Pictures and now in the AFI Collection give us a chance to look closely at the work of a formerly unsung artist. Others await their rediscovery.]

Famous Players-Lasky 1921
Director: William C. de Mille.
Adaptation: Clara Beranger, based on the novel and play by Zona Gale.
Cast: Lois Wilson, Milton Sills, Theodore Roberts, Helen Ferguson, Mabel Van Buren, Clarence Burton.

William de Mille's identity is largely eclipsed, not only by the scarcity of surviving prints, but by the exceedingly luminous career of his younger brother Cecil B. Cecil differed from William in many ways — the most superficial of them being that Cecil spelled De Mille with a capital "D" and William employed the lower case. Superficial — but symptomatic. Where Cecil was given to the grandiose, William preferred the intimate. Where Cecil was known for his hellfire and brimstone — both on the screen and on the set — William was softer-spoken, easier-going, and perhaps more humanistic. *Miss Lulu Bett*, one of William de Mille's surviving films in The American Film Institute Collection, displays these qualities to perfection. . . .

The film is relatively free of the posturing and exaggeration that plagued much of the silent cinema. Griffith's greatest weakness, perhaps, was the cloying saintliness of his heroines — a vision of virginity that must have seemed incredible even in its own time. De Mille's heroine, Miss Lulu Bett, described as a "timid soul" in the titles, is nevertheless a believable character — a three-dimensional woman. De Mille's film has emotional power, yet it refuses to wallow in sentiment. It is alert to the small details that define characters and relationships, and the director was able to convey them with delicacy and tact. In an era of overstatement, he managed not to say too much — but rather, just enough.

The screenplay for *Miss Lulu Bett* was written by Clara Beranger, who was de Mille's wife, and there is obvious harmony between the written film and de Mille's interpretation. De Mille was a writer himself. Before going to Hollywood, he'd written such plays as "The Warrens of Virginia" and "Strongheart." He also wrote screenplays for his brother Cecil, including "The Woman God Forgot" and "Temptation." And he helped Cecil launch a wave of semi-sophisticated sex romps in the twenties with *Why Change Your Wife?*

Miss Lulu Bett is a film that reflects genuine care and attention to detail. Beranger adapted it from a novel and play by Zona Gale. Lois Wilson plays the role of Miss Lulu Bett, described in the titles as "the family beast of burden, whose timid soul has failed to break the bonds of family servitude." She lives with her sister, brother-in-law, and mother in an all-American household that is something of a mess. Her brother-in-law, Dwight Deacon (Theodore Roberts), is a pompous oaf; his wife is a supplicative ninny (Mabel Van Buren) who calls him "Dwightie." An older and younger daughter and Lulu's mother also contribute to the household miseries.

The film establishes its theme — but doesn't really summarize itself — with the three opening titles: "The greatest tragedy in the world, because it is the most frequent, is that of a human soul caught in the toils of the commonplace. . . . This happens in many a home where family ties, which could be bonds of love, have become iron fetters of dependence. . . . If you want to know what kind of family lives in a house, look at the dining room."

The first shots in the film, of course, are of the dining room. The family is then introduced. Lulu is first seen working at the family stove. It quickly becomes apparent that Miss Lulu Bett is a virtual slave in the house — because she has nowhere else to go. When Dwight's brother Ninian (Clarence Burton) returns home from South America after twenty years and takes the family to dinner, he laughingly goes through a mock marriage ceremony with Miss Lulu Bett. It seems like just a tasteless joke until the father declares, "Say, we forgot I'm a justice of the peace." and the marriage is therefore valid. For lack of something better to do with her life, and for the hope of getting away from the oppressive Deacons, the girl decides she might as well be married, even to this dude. The marriage ends — Ninian, it turns out, already was married to someone else — and Lulu is faced with the humiliation of returning home just seven days later. But "for the whole week," note the titles, she knew "jthe joy of having someone treat her kindly," and this will eventually contribute to her liberation, when she asserts her independence, leaves the Deacons, and at last rewards the amorous advanced of stalwart schoolteacher Neil Cornish (Milton Sills).

Liberation is somewhat the theme of the film (today it might be called "The Liberation of Miss L.B."). Coincidentally, Miss Lulu raises one of the issues of semantics lately advanced by Women's Lib when she first meets Ninian:

He: "Is it 'Miss' or ''Mrs.'?

She: "'Miss.' From choice. What kind of a Mister are you — a 'Miss Mister' or a 'Mrs. Mister'?"

He: "That's right — a man's name don't tell you if he's married, does it?"

Let the records show that the issue came up in 1921.

Throughout the film, Lois Wilson's performance, under de Mille's alert direction, conspicuously avoids the pathetic. The role might indeed have turned into a cross between Cinderella and Little Eva. But when Lulu announces at one point, "I still have my pride," we believe her, because she, Beranger, and de Mille have given the character dignity.

Similarly, the Deacon family, though hardly a collection of heroes, isn't a set of stock villains, either. De Mille stops short of making them too onerous. Small things contribute to the portrait — as when father insists that dinner is late until his watch is proven wrong by the 6 o'clock factory whistle sounding in the distance. He claims then that the whistle must be wrong, that it's a trick to get more work out of the men. We recognize in this behavior the symptoms of common pomposity — not villainy.

Peripheral details are helpful, too. At the city restaurant, a quartet of high-lifers stir their drinks with flower stems — a fresh image of affluent decadence. When a local suitor named Bobby plans an elopement, de Mille catches the panic all over his face. When the elopement attempt is thwarted (by the clear-thinking Miss Lulu Bett), Bobby remembers to cash in the two train tickets he will no longer be needing. De Mille's treatment of the burgeoning romance between Lulu and the schoolteacher is deft and non-cloying. At the end of the film, in the teacher's classroom, a student has scrawled, "Teacher loves L---" on the blackboard. To show Lulu how he feels — still maintaining a discreet distance — the teacher completes the sentence, and then writes, "Does Lulu love me?" She writes the letter "Y" and, before she can complete the word, they kiss.

Crucial also to the film is de Mille's sense of period Americana. It permeates the interior scenes at the Deacon house, but surfaces most notably in a scene outside the church on the Sunday after Miss Lulu Bett has returned from her unsuccessful marriage. The subject of the sermon has been "charity of heart," but as soon as they're out the door of the building, the women and men divide into groups and gossip. "Her husband got tired of her and sent her home," jabber the women. "If a feller leaves his bride after one week, it don't say much for the bride," gloat the men. The teacher stands up to this small-town Puritan ritual by offering Lulu a ride home in his crank-up car. The women scoff that men invariably chase after "a woman who ain't regular." The sequence conveys something sanguine about provincial mores and basic middle-class values.

The whole film conveys a great deal. And one of its most obvious revelations is that William de Mille may be one of the true unsung poets of the silent screen. When film preservationists can contribute toward the restoration or overdue establishment of a reputation like de Mille's, they perform a service both to the art and to the artists. William de Mille was, from available evidence, just such an artist.

Miss Lulu Bett

RONALD BOWERS
Manslaughter

Review reprinted from Frank N. Magill, Magill's Survey of
Cinema: *Silent Films (Salem Press, 1982).*

Released: 1922
Production: Cecil B. De Mille for Famous Players-Lasky; released
by Paramount
Direction: Cecil B. De Mille
Screenplay: Jeanie Macpherson; based on the novel by Alice
Duer Miller
Cinematography: Alvin Wyckoff and L. Guy Wilky
Editing: Anne Bauchens
Set decoration: Paul Iribe
Length: 10 reels/9,061 feet

Principal characters:

Daniel O'Bannon	Thomas Meighan
Lydia Thorne	Leatrice Joy
Evans, her maid	Lois Wilson
Governor Stephen Albee	John Miltern
Judge Homans	George Fawcett
Mrs. Drummond	Julia Faye

Among the themes which Cecil B. De Mille's silent films encom-
passed was the idea of there being one set of laws for the rich and
another for the poor. He had explored this theme brilliantly in *Male
and Female* (1919), the film version of Sir James M. Barrie's play *The
Admirable Crichton,* which expressed the view that the caste system
in English society was permanently established and unbreakable
except in times of extreme emergency, and then would automatically and absolutely revert to its former guise after the emergency.

Male and Female dealt with the world of master and servant, and
De Mille pursued that theme once again in *Saturday Night* (1922). In
that film, a debutante is engaged to a young man of her own social
position but falls in love with her chauffeur and marries him.
Concurrently, her fiance falls for the daughter of his family's laun-
dress and marries her. Both marriages fail, end in divorce, and in
the last reel, the four young people are rematched with the partners
from their own social backgrounds, thus showing that the rules of
life are established and cannot be transgressed.

It is a cynical point of view but one over which revolutions have been fought, and De Mille, whom many called an absolute cynic, knew this theme was one to which the filmgoing public would respond. It was his ability to discover the lowest common denominator of public taste, and if his detractors made fun of his lack of artistic merit, De Mille simply went ahead and made his pictures "for the people."

In his book, *The Parade's Gone By*, Kevin Brownlow quotes veteran journalist/screenwriter Adela Rogers St. Johns as describing De Mille as "one hundred per cent cynical. . . . There wasn't a moment when he wasn't acting. he was so good a ham he could sell anything." This combination of ham, cynic, and showman had earned De Mille his reputation as a director who was sure-fire at the box office. His remarkable directorial talents as displayed in *The Cheat* (1915) and *Male and Female* among others, additionally made him a force with which to be reckoned. As the 1920's progressed, however, and the overall result of his films continued to present his notorious combination of sex, sadism, and moralizing, he began to decline as a viable director.

Manslaughter, neither as good as some think nor as deplorable as his detractors would have one believe, was the film which best marks the end of the innovative period in De Mille's career. It reveals some of his best and worst traits as a filmmaker and presages his decline into simply a circus showman, king of the spectaculars.

The film is based on a novel by Alice Duer Miller which appeared in the *Saturday Evening Post*. De Mille read it and asked Jesse L. Lasky to buy it for him. It is the story of Lydia Thorne (Leatrice Joy), a rich society girl who is one of the jazz crazy, thrill-seeking pretty young things of the post-World War I era. While recklessly driving her roadster convertible a motorcycle cop tries to arrest her; she speeds up and races him only to have his cycle hit her automobile. The policeman's body flies into the air and lands across the hood of her car, killing him. The policeman had just been honored for saving the lives of some children, and when his wife arrives at the scene of the accident, she places the chevrons which he had just earned on his sleeve and salutes him. Lydia sobs in remorse at this touching scene which is the result of her carelessness.

Arrested and brought to trial, Lydia is prosecuted by Daniel O'Bannon (Thomas Meighan), the young district attorney to whom she is engaged. The upstanding O'Bannon adamantly preaches that there is too often one set of laws for the rich and another for the poor, and he believes that the only way for Lydia to find salvation is to serve a just sentence in prison.

In one scene, O'Bannon compares the reckless ways of today's youth with that of the kind of behavior which caused the fall of Rome and here, in typically excessive De Mille style, appears an all-out Roman orgy. With elaborate sets, near naked dancing girls, and gladiators, De Mille pulls out all the stops in giving his escape-seeking audience a taste of the pleasure-seeking ways of hedonism. In this flashback, Joy appears as the Roman empress who hosts the orgy and Meighan plays the chief of the Barbarians who sack Rome.

Continuing the story, once Lydia is convicted and sent to prison, the weight of his decision in having her convicted rests heavily on O'Bannon's mind, breaks his spirit, and drives him to drink.

In prison, Lydia discovers a side of life, a harshness and cruelty, she never knew existed. At first, in her typical spoiled manner, she is bitter, but finally she sees the errors of her ways and vows to reform. She discovers that another of her inmates is her former maid, Evans (Lois Wilson), who has been arrested and jailed for stealing Lydia's jewelry. Lydia has by now so changed from the rich, spoiled brat that she was, that she is able honestly and democratically to become friends with Evans. Lydia becomes a model prisoner and even accepts the degradation of having to scrub floors. When she is finally released from jail after serving a one-year sentence, Lydia and Evans open a soup kitchen, rehabilitate O'Bannon, and help him run for governor. True love overcomes even political ambitions, however, and O'Bannon abandons politics and marries Lydia.

In preparation for the film, screenwriter Jeanie Macpherson decided she should experience prison life at first hand in order to create a sense of realism in those scenes. She arranged to go to Detroit where she knew that the Detroit House of Detention incarcerated petty criminals with killers. She arranged to be arrested for stealing a furpiece (from a friend) and, as planned, was caught and jailed along with hardened criminals. After three days of lice, horrible food, and watching female prisoners fight and/or have sex with each other, she arranged her release, and upon arriving back in California, tearfully fell in the arms of De Mille, saying she had never experienced anything so horrible. When the film was released, the prison scenes were praised for exactly the sense of reality for which Macpherson had striven. Both the acting of Leatrice Joy and Lois Wilson in these scenes, as well as the prison sets, which had been designed by Paul Iribe, earned words of tribute.

The film was billed as "A Drama of the Mad Age! Is the Modern World Racing to Ruin on a Wave of Jazz and Cocktails?"; and De Mille was in a way preaching against the fast-living habits of an immoral society. Some feel, however, that he was just cynical enough to add the preachment so he might have the artistic freedom, and the poetic license, to film his elaborate Roman orgy.

It is curious that 1922, the year after the film was released, was also the year that Will H. Hays became president of the Motion Picture Producers and Distributors Association of America and vowed to crack down on the immoral aspects of the motion-picture industry both on and off the screen. This followed the sensationalism of the notorious trial of Fatty Arbuckle, accused of the rape murder of starlet Virginia Rappe. Certainly, De Mille regarded this act as an intrusion into the filmmaker's freedom of expression, so he, by necessity, had to envelope his sex, sadism, and titillation in the polite framework of morality, thus giving the cynic the last word.

Joy had appeared in the lesser De Mille opus, *Saturday Night.*, and was now the star of *Manslaughter*. Beautiful and talented, she was then the wife of John Gilbert and had come to De Mille's attention through her Goldwyn films. He envisioned her as a replacement for Gloria Swanson in his films, for Swanson, with his consent, had gone on to better things. Joy appeared in two more De Mille vehicles: she was the young girl in the modern sequence of *The Ten Commandments* (1923) and an opera star in *Triumph* (1924).

While criticized for the spectacle excesses of the Roman orgy sequence, *Manslaughter* earned praise for its modern story and for the acting of both Joy and Wilson. The film cost $380,000 to make and, proving De Mille right once again, earned $1,200,000. *Manslaughter* was remade twice: once in 1930 with Fredric March and Claudette Colbert and again in 1936 under the title *And Sudden Death* starring Randolph Scott and Frances Drake.

ROB EDELMAN
The Marriage Circle

Review reprinted from Frank N. Magill, Magill's Survey of Cinema: Silent Films (Salem Press, 1982).

Released: 1924
Production: Warner Bros.
Direction: Ernst Lubitsch
Assistant direction: James Flood and Henry Blanke
Screenplay: Paul Bern; based on the play Nurein Traum (Only a Dream) by Lothar Schmidt
Cinematography: Charles Van Enger
Length: 8 reels/8,200 feet

Principal characters:

Charlotte Braun	Florence Vidor
Dr. Franz Braun	Monte Blue
Mizzi Stock	Marie Prevost
Dr. Gustav Mueller	Creighton Hale
Professor Josef Stock	Adolphe Menjou
Detective	Harry Myers
Neurotic patient	Dale Fuller
Miss Hofer	Esther Ralston

The cinema of Ernst Lubitsch is special and unique. He directed almost thirty films in America, most of which could never have been made by a native because he infused them with European wit, manners, and sophistication as only a continental could. Born in Berlin in 1892, Lubitsch directed shorts and features in Germany between 1915 and 1923 before coming to the United States. His second film in his new country, and his most famous silent, is *The Marriage Circle* (1924).

The film is set in Vienna in the first years of the twentieth century. Professor Josef Stock (Adolphe Menjou) and his wife Mizzi (Marie Prevost) have recently moved to the city. They are unhappily married, and the film opens with a scene showing them squabbling. The Professor tries to put on a sock, but his big toe protrudes from a large hole, and he has no more in his drawer. Mizzi's drawer, however, is crammed with stockings, all neatly arranged. Later, when he attaches a small mirror to a window in order to shave, she selfishly pushes him aside.

Mizzi receives a letter from her best friend, Charlotte Braun (Florence Vidor), chastising her for not visiting since arriving in Vienna. When Mizzi enters a taxi on the way to see her friend, by coincidence it has already been engaged by Charlotte's new husband, Dr. Franz Braun (Monte Blue), a fashionable physician whom Mizzi has never met. The strangers agree to share the cab, and Josef observes them drive away together as he shaves. He smiles as he sees them, thinking that this might potentially develop into an excuse for a divorce.

The racy, temperamental Mizzi is attracted to the doctor and tries to capture his attention. As the taxi turns, she almost falls into his lap, and she inches closer to him to look in a mirror on his side of the cab. Franz, who is deeply in love with his wife, is bothered by Mizzi's actions, so he asks the driver to stop, and he leaves. Mizzi powders her face and rearranges a chair so that the doctor will be forced to sit near her. Franz takes Mizzi's pulse, and she responds by holding his wrist. Josef enters and notices the contact. The home lives of the Stocks and Brauns are now contrasted: the former sit at opposite ends of the table when eating breakfast, while the latter embrace. The unperturbed Mizzi next visits Franz's office, again attempting to seduce him. Franz's partner, Dr. Gustav Mueller (Creighton Hale), arrives and observes the doctor's back and a woman's arm around his neck. He assumes it is Charlotte and is then surprised to find her outside in the waiting room. Gustav is secretly delighted, because he himself is in love with Charlotte.

The Brauns hold a dinner party, and Franz rearranges the place cards so that he will not be seated next to Mizzi. Charlotte, at Mizzi's urging, thinks her husband has a crush on an attractive blond, Miss Hofer (Esther Ralston), and has changed the seating arrangements to sit near her; thus, she switches the cards back to their original places with her husband next to her friend. Charlotte confides to Mizzi her fears about Franz's feelings for Miss Hofer and requests that her friend keep the doctor preoccupied. Mizzi then switches the place cards a third time, and Charlotte is angered at the final seating arrangement. She glares at her husband and purposely flirts with Gustav.

Mizzi dances with Franz, while Charlotte does the same with Gustav, then Mizzi maneuvers her partner outside, into a garden. When they are seated on a bench, she wraps her arm around his leg, puckers her lips expectantly, and tosses away her scarf. Charlotte and Gustav enter the garden and see Franz's foot dragging the scarf. Charlotte knows it is Mizzi's, who by now has been abandoned by

Franz, who in turn is now on the terrace, innocently conversing with Miss Hofer.

Mizzi passes a note to Franz, explaining that she will wait for him in a taxi after the party. He tears it up but meets her anyway after the angry Charlotte throws him out of the house. Charlotte is sorry, however, so she closes her eyes to kiss her husband, but mistakenly kisses Gustav instead. When she realizes her error, she orders Gustav to leave. Meanwhile, Mizzi again fails to seduce Franz.

Josef, by this time, has enough evidence against his wife and orders her to leave their house; then he confronts Franz, who denies his part in the affair. Charlotte visits Mizzi at her hotel in an effort to console her friend, who meanwhile has requested that Franz also come to see her. Franz and Charlotte accidentally meet in Mizzi's room, and Charlotte realizes her husband is the "guilty party." As he declares his innocence, Charlotte admits her flirtation with Gustav, so both are equally to blame, and they can be reconciled. Gustav then passes Mizzi, who is riding in a cab. She waves to him, and as the film closes, he sets out to join her.

The Marriage Circle is the first of Lubitsch's sly, urbane, nonchalant social comedy-satires. The director claimed that Charles Chaplin's *A Woman of Paris* (1923, and also featuring Adolphe Menjou, as the "richest bachelor in Paris") as his source of inspiration, and *The Marriage Circle* seems at times to satirize the Chaplin film. *A Woman of Paris* was a moralistic tale of a country girl (Edna Purviance) who thinks that she has been jilted by her art student boyfriend, travels to Paris, becomes the mistress of the frivolous Menjou character, but eventually leaves him and Paris to return to the country. Lubitsch imbues his film with an air of cynicism in that he depicts the state of marriage as a never-ending cycle of love obliterated by time, of love inexorably destroyed and replaced by antagonism and hatred.

On the surface, the two relationships in *The Marriage Circle* are completely opposite. The marriages are best personified by the shots of the couples at their respective breakfast tables. The Stocks tolerate each other at best; their involvement with each other is based on self-indulgence, lies, and manipulation. this is apparent from the opening sequence onward. Conversely, the Brauns are naively in love. Charlotte consoles her best friend, who is heartlessly scheming to steal her husband; Franz gallantly deflects Mizzi's passes, but in the end cannot avoid being "found out" by his wife. The Stocks have been married longer than the Brauns; obviously, they cared for each other early in their relationship, perhaps as much as do Charlotte and Franz, but something has come between them — maybe, only time — and they now despise each other. Charlotte and Franz' problems are caused by their constant overreaction to situations; in particular, Charlotte allows herself to become jealous of Miss Hofer and then flirts with Gustav to get even. At the finale, their misunderstanding is resolved, but one wonders how many misunderstandings will occur before their relationship again deteriorates. As the title indicates, Lubitsch sees marriage as cyclical, and thus, it is predictable that Charlotte and Franz will end as Mizzi and Josef. According to Lubitsch, marriage is not necessarily the happy-ever-after state presented and taken for granted in so many other motion pictures.

The Marriage Circle is expertly cast. Menjou is at his best in a role tailor-made for his talents. Florence Vidor, Monte Blue, and Marie Prevost, all popular silent stars, and Creighton Hale, who played sophisticated first and second leads during the 1920's, are all superior. The actresses in particular are at the zenith of their respective careers. The film received stunning reviews, and if it no longer seems original, it is because the formula has been repeated so often with varying degrees of success by Lubitsch and other filmmakers in the last sixty years.

The film was one of the all-time favorites of George Jean Nathan, Akira Kurosawa, and Chaplin (who wrote of Lubitsch in his autobiography, "He could do more to show the grace and humor of sex in a nonlustful way than any other director I've ever heard of"). It was also Alfred Hitchcock's favorite Lubitsch work and was named to *The New York Times* ten best films of the year list. Both *The Marriage Circle* and *A Woman of Paris* immediately inspired a series of mediocre domestic comedies made by such directors as Harry d'Abbadie d'Arrast (Chaplin's assistant on *A Woman of Paris*), Richard Rosson, Monta Bell, Malcolm St. Clair, and Roy Del Ruth. Lubitsch himself went on to make other films similar to *The Marriage Circle*, such as *Three Women* (1924), *Forbidden Paradise* (1924), *Kiss Me Again* (1925), *Lady Windermere's Fan* (1925), and *So This Is Paris* (1926), often using the same cast. He remade *The Marriage Circle* with sound in 1932 as *One Hour with You*, but in that film he focused solely on the "good couple" (Maurice Chevalier and Jeanette MacDonald), whose relationship is upset by the arrival of coquettish Mitzi Olivier (Genevieve Tobin). In *One Hour with You*, the characters also talk directly to the camera, and the film is certainly more fun than *The Marriage Circle*, but it also seems more trivial and is not the cornerstone that is the original.

ARTHUR LENNIG
Dancing Mothers

Review from Classics of the Film (*Madison, Wisconsin Film Society Press, 1965*) by Arthur Lennig

(U.S.A., 1926)
Directed and produced by Herbert Brenon
Script by Forrest Halsey from the play, *Dancing Mothers*, by
Edgar Selwyn and Edmund Goulding
Starring: Alice Joyce (Mrs. Ethel Westcourt), Clara Bow
(Kittens), Conway Tearle (Gerald "Jerry" Naughton), Dorothy
Cumming (Mrs. Mazzarene), Norman Trevor (Hugh Westcourt)
Note: The play opened on August 11, 1924 and featured Helen
Hayes as Kittens.

Social movements cannot always be pinpointed in time, but
between 1915 and 1925 a revolution took place in the United States.
Some people blamed it on the war, the anarchists, the League of
Nations, the automobile, and the movies. But, whatever the cause,
the revolution occurred. The good old days of high morals and low
skirts, of calling cards and cutaway coats and afternoon teas vanished. Victorian mannerisms and concepts of women as "Little Dear
Ones," in short, the whole tradition of Puritanism, dissolved in a
wispy cloud of a woman's cigarette and in the strong breath of
bootleg booze. The young maiden smelling of rose petals and
blushing at the slightest hint of reality soon reeked of perfume and
talked of Freudian repressions and phallic symbolism. America
entered the twentieth century late, but it entered with a vengeance.

The shock of the war, the let-down after the peace treaty, the
problems of "How're you gonna keep them down on the farm," the
loss of the pioneer spirit, and Harding's "normalcy" had their effect.
The post-war theme came to be "Let's live it up." Jazz and bathtub
gin bestowed danger and drama on the simple act of drinking and
dancing. Everyone, it seemed, was having a helluva good time. And
the drive to have as much fun as possible — "you're only young
once —" caught on.

The films illustrated these rapidly changing views and indeed
contributed to them. Back in 1914 in *A Fool There Was* Theda Bara
played the vamp, the evil temptress. But this naive concept that a
woman to be good in bed must have some allegiance with the devil

or the dark forces eventually disappeared. The opposite of Theda Bara was Mary Pickford who represented the good sweet girl whose entire favors might consist of no more than a peck on the cheek. But men wanted more than this; they wanted at least the promise of sex, if not the sex itself. They wanted to feel dangerous, even if they were not.

Conversely, the women too began to demand more. They grew tired of looking like someone's kid sister. They wanted to lure, to be sexy, to be a *femme fatale*. Other women, too demure to act out such a modern role, still had their desires and secret needs. These longings were answered by Rudolph Valentino who became the symbol of the expert lover. Everybody knew he was once a gigolo. He brought adventure and romance to what frigid women and inept husbands had made into an unimaginative habit. He acted out the dreams of every frustrated girl. In his role of the sheik he carries away a protesting woman and introduces her to the pleasures of love. The psychological mechanism of this initiation is obvious. The woman (who wants really to be ravished) is taken forcibly by her lover (the force thus removing the burden of having to consent and comply) and thus she is allowed to enjoy sex without any guilt.

As sex came to the forefront of American life, battle lines soon appeared. Parents and teachers and clergy (the three big institutions of stodginess) came out against the fast and wicked life; the youngsters came out for it. And so the cries went up of "degenerate" on one side and "oldfashioned" on the other.

Of course a compromise developed. A new group of conventions came into being. Although the girl wanted to "live," she still remained good: a little shop-worn, perhaps, but still not second-hand. And the establishment, though not approving, began to tolerate the freer and easier life. The popular arts (magazines, theatre and, of course, the movies) soon reflected this new code of behavior. The conflict between the two generations became resolved: the young grew less wild and the old less straight-laced. And a happy ending was enjoyed by all.

Dancing Mothers, in spite of its dreadful title, reflects the tensions and problems of this era. Based on a Broadway play which opened in August, 1924, the film deals with the collapse of the old moral structure and the growth of the new urge to "live":

> The woman sacrifices her youth to be a wife and mother, and just when she has reached the age when her duties have ended and life lies before her, you say it is over — the Divine Will commands her to resign all thoughts of further living. That's fair — that's very just — isn't it?

This speech from the play sums up the problem of the modern mother, but a problem which was already growing trite, Arthur Hornblow, the reviewer for *Theatre Arts* in an October 1924 article said about the Broadway production:

> Its theme is conventional and shop-worn; its situations threadbare and hackneyed, yet an unexpected twist at the end saved it from being utterly commonplace and is likely to carry it to success.

What appeared as an "unexpected twist" to an experienced theatre critic must have seemed the height of audacity in Hollywood and yet, somehow, this unconventional ending was allowed to remain along with much of the action and many of the major speeches (as titles, of course.) Indeed, the film survives as one of Hollywood's more forthright efforts in dealing with reality.

The film concerns three people: a father, mother, and daughter and their attempts to cope with life and convention. As the film opens, the daughter (Kittens) and her father (Mr. Westcourt) are returning from a pleasure trip to Europe. Aboard ship she meets Jerry Naughton, a man-about-town. Later, upon docking, Kittens tells her still attractive mother (a former stage star) that she wouldn't have enjoyed the voyage because she was too "old-fashioned." A few weeks later when Mrs. Westcourt complains to her husband about Kittens' frequent dating, Mr. Westcourt announces that the youngster of today can take care of herself. Kittens is pursuing Jerry Naughton. At a wild night club, she leaves her rather innocent beau in order to dance with Jerry while across the room her philandering father is slipping some money to his current mistress.

While the husband and daughter chase around enjoying themselves, the mother spends her evenings at home. Her friend, a Countess (Old World Sophistication) drops by one night and says that she no longer wastes her time foolishly staying home alone. The Countess states that she has a few good years left and that she is going to make use of them. Convinced, Mrs. Westcourt decides to do the town.

Her decision to go to a night club, however, seems to come more from desperation than from any wish to enjoy herself. At the club she tries to forget her past by giving her maiden name and adopting a French accent. She meets Jerry there and as she sits down at the table with him, she pushes a flower in a vase impetuously away from the center of the table so they can converse better. This small detail reveals her eagerness and spirit. Soon after, she makes a date with Jerry ostensibly so that he will not pay further attention to

Kittens but also because she too is rather interested. She toasts, "I'm playing with life." But her husband arrives and, shocked by her presence, tells his wife to come home now or not at all. But she stays. After numerous meetings, Jerry has fallen in love with Mrs. Westcourt and has invited her to his place for a drink. Meantime, Kittens, spurned, shows up at Jerry's apartment, forces her way in past the valet, and begins to get drunk. When Mrs. Westcourt telephones to refuse the invitation, she hears her child's voice, and shows up at the apartment to save her from Jerry's seductive ways. But when she arrives the daughter has vanished. Jerry is delighted with Mrs. Westcourt's arrival and tells her that "For the first time in my life I'm sincere with a woman." But she doesn't answer, saying merely that she does not want to see him again. (Notice that Mrs. Westcourt maintains her virtue and her goodness by not wishing to get involved; it is only fate — that is, her wish to save her daughter — that brings her to his apartment. That she is not portrayed at all as being really anxious to have an affair shows that the film, like the play, still adheres to the old virtues.)

But while she is telling Jerry she does not wish to see him, her daughter (who has not left, but has hidden in the next room) enters and brattishly accuses her mother of stealing her beau. Soon after, Mr. Westcourt arrives and Mrs. Westcourt sarcastically remarks that it is the first time the family has been together in a long time. With true Victorian fervor, Mr. Westcourt indignantly tells his wife. "You may consider yourself free." The mother does not beg forgiveness. A moment later all three of the Westcourts leave. As Jerry looks out the window, an overhead camera shot shows two cars pull away in opposite directions, an economical way of pointing out that the mother does not return home.

A few days later, after telling Jerry she must never see him again, Mrs. Westcourt arrives at home to pick up her clothing; she is going to Europe (apparently the geographical symbol of "living"). The father asks her to stay, but she refuses. Then Kittens comes out and tells her father that she will convince her mother. "Leave it to me," she says confidently. The daughter begins to plead. "Won't you stay, Mumsey?" At this point the film hovers on the brink of a sentimental ending, but it avoids this pitfall when the mother realizes that Kittens only wants her to stay for selfish reasons. The last shot of the film shows her car driving away. Like Ibsen's Nora in *The Doll's House*, the wife actually leaves her meaningless marriage to start her life anew. She will, as the film implies, now attempt to "live."

This film is unconventional not only in the ending. The usual pattern would have Kittens be a charming, sweet, lovable kid with a heart of gold, but she is different. She's brattish, spoiled, inelegant, and a bit boorish. Not knowing how to drink or woo, she does both to excess by getting drunk and by forcing her way into Jerry's apartment. Kittens, however, is by no means villainous, but rather a spoiled and selfish girl — unusual only in that this realistic characterization so seldom appears on the screen.

Her mother, to the contrary, is a lady, but a lady with the courage of her convictions. She has tolerated her husband's absences for a long time before she ventures out on her own and, even when she does, she is not really intending any affair.

Thus *Dancing Mothers* opposes the hypocrisy of a loveless marriage and argues courageously (for its time) that life should be lived, not merely endured. When this film is compared with many of the same period and even with those of more modern times, one realizes how brave it is for "official" American morals demanded (just as they still do) that the home be maintained and that anyone having or thinking of having an adulterous affair must be punished in some way or other.

Dancing Mothers merits attention as an example of American attitudes towards "living it up," night clubs, philandering husbands, and general, though somewhat tame, libertinism. Although some critics might call it a soap-opera (true, there are no profound moments), the film does attempt to deal with real, though somewhat muted, issues. Besides being a sociological document of the Jazz Age, it is also an interesting example of good story telling. The director, Herbert Brenon, is not arty, but tells a story quickly, efficiently, and clearly. His handling of the involved entrances and exits, the acting of the players, the pace, all reveal excellent craftsmanship and show what the above average, but by no means extraordinary, film of the twenties was like. As a period piece of both subject and technique, the film bears revival.

AUDREY KUPFERBERG
The Grand Duchess and the Waiter

Review reprinted from Frank N. Magill, *Magill's Survey of Cinema: Silent Films (Salem Press, 1982).*

Released: 1926
Production: Adolph Zukor and Jesse L. Lasky for Famous Players-Lasky; released by Paramount
Direction: Malcolm St. Clair
Screenplay: Pierre Collings; based on John Lynch's adaptation of *La Grandduchesse et le garcon d'etage* by Alfred Savoir
Cinematography: Lee Garmes
Length: 7 reels/6,314 feet

Principal characters:
Albert Belfort . . . . Aldolphe Menjou
The Grand Duchess Zenia . . . . Florence Vidor
The Grand Duke Peter . . . . Andre Beranger
The Grand Duke Paul . . . . Lawrence Grant
The Countess Prascovia Avaloff . . . . . . Dot Farley

In the mid-1920's, American filmgoers delighted in viewing a genre of comedy which depicted marital unrest with a lighthearted, continental flair. It is understandable that the post-World War I, "jazz-mad" generation would flock to films portraying love and marriage in a worldly manner. The genre might not have developed, however, had it not been for the initial success of Ernst Lubitsch's comedy of manners, *The Marriage Circle*, in 1924. On the heels of this witty tale, Famous Players-Lasky/Paramount and Warner Bros. generated a succession of films satirizing life among the wealthy, principally directed by Lubitsch, Malcolm St. Clair, Paul Bern, and Harry d'Abbadie d'Arrast.

The Grand Duchess and the Waiter, one of the finest examples of this genre, was selected as one of *The New York Times'* ten best films for 1926, and is possibly the best conceived project of St. Clair's prolific career. One of the few silent-film directors born in Los Angeles, St. Clair entered the industry as a bit player and gag writer for Mack Sennett in 1915, while still in his teens. He directed comedy shorts for a few years, followed by a brief fling with action pictures. Then came *Are Parents People?* in 1925; with this film he proved he could direct society comedy. With the subsequent release of *The* could direct society comedy. With the subsequent release of *The Grand Duchess and the Waiter* in February, 1926, he established himself as a leading director of sophisticated comedy films.

To characterize the genre, one need only examine the components of *The Grand Duchess and the Waiter*. A romance of society folk is unraveled through an enjoyable series of unorthodox adventures of the naughty-but-fun ilk. Adolphe Menjou plays a rich society playboy, and it is interesting to note that this Pittsburg-born performer acts the debonair lead role in almost every major film of the genre, starting with *The Marriage Circle*. The story is set in Paris, a city so magical to American audiences that all disbelief is suspended whenever the events occur there. To intensify the excitement, this particular screenplay is based on a play actually written by a Frenchman and performed in Paris in 1924.

The Grand Duchess and the Waiter opens on "a June night in Paris — an ancient city with delightfully young ideas." A group of *bons vivants* at the ballet are awaiting the arrival of their friend Albert Belfort (Adolphe Menjou), who has been detained by "business affairs." The scene cuts to Albert kissing the hand of a woman with whom he definitely had not attended a business conference.

Inside the theater, the Grand Duchess Zenia (Florence Vidor) watches the ballet. She has "sought shelter in France from the storms of revolution in her native Russia." Her arms are strewn with jewels. Having joined his friends inside the theater. Albert spies Zenia through opera glasses, is smitten by her beauty, and sends her his card requesting an introduction. Had this film intended merely to tell a tale, she would simply have torn up the card, but *The Grand Duchess and the Waiter* is a stylized comedy of manners. In that tradition, the card is first handed to one of her male companions, then to her second male companion who is about to tear it up. Zenia then takes the card, reads it, and tears it up. She and her entourage leave the ballet without acknowledging Albert.

In the belief that their exile may be nearly over, the group returns to the Hotel St. Antoine. Albert follows and learns from the hotel manager Zenia's identity and the fact that she and her entourage are in the royal suite. "Her country is a republic now but she refuses to know it," says the manager. Albert engages the rooms directly below the royal suite. From this point in the film, the drama revolves on action within these suites and interaction of the two suites caused by a chandelier in Albert's room which sways whenever someone paces upstairs.

In the royal suite, a telegram arrives from Ivan of Odessa. "The revolution continues disastrously. We hold no hope for your return to power. Send money immediately. We are destitute." Zenia paces the floor, the chandelier in the room below sways, and Albert blows a kiss upward.

Albert telephones Zenia, but the Grand Duke Peter (Andre Beranger) speaks to him; then the Grand Duke Paul (Lawrence Grant) speaks to him; finally, her companion the Countess Prascovia Avaloff (Dot Farley) speaks to him, then they hang up the telephone. Standing up to the challenge, Albert telephones his valet Charles and orders his belongings moved to the Hotel St. Antoine. Arriving the next morning, Charles asks, "What brings us here, sir?" to which Albert responds, "Love, Charles, love! But it's *real* love this time, Charles."

The inhabitants of the royal suite are not as elated as Albert. The hotel bill for the suite which occupies the entire third floor is unpaid. The champagne Peter consumes has skyrocketed to a sum of 4,453 francs, and Paul's cigars cost 259 francs. The bill totals 275,420.90 francs, and the royal family has no money. Peter explains that he tried to earn money by buying automobiles on credit and selling them cheaper for cash, but the police objected. Paul, paces the room, and the chandelier sways in the room below. Albert, seated directly under the chandelier, looks up from his breakfast to throw a kiss. The hotel waiter says, "It's the Duchess," because he has the honor of waiting on her daily, a job Albert says he would relish.

That afternoon Albert dresses in the uniform of a hotel waiter to serve tea to the royal suite. Inside the suite, however, trouble is brewing. The hotel manager has come to collect the bill, and Zenia must sell Catherine the Great's necklace to meet expenses. Albert serves tea in a most conspicuous manner, and, when Zenia announces that "the tea is vile," Albert agrees. Albert is so clumsy that the royal family assures him that if he were in Russia he would be flogged. As Albert cleans the mess he has made of afternoon tea, Zenia smiles. Albert must ask Prascovia if he can continue to serve the Grand Duchess, and she says no. Zenia intervenes, however, saying, "We are touched by this man's expression of loyalty. We will give him another chance." At that moment, Albert almost drops the samovar and succeeds in breaking several plates.

Prascovia warns Zenia that it is a mistake to keep Albert in their service, that possibly he is in love with her. Laughing, Zenia replies, "Ridiculous, a waiter in love with a grand duchess!" Peter, too, laughs and then summons Albert to Zenia, at her request. Zenia pretends to be asleep, and Albert descends to one knee and kisses her foot. She jumps up and roars, "To the salt mines of Siberia!" Albert runs from the room and is stopped by Prascovia who asks him where he is going. "To Siberia for some salt," he says. Zenia calls him back for punishment: she will have him perform all her services personally.

Back in his rooms after a hard day as a waiter, he sleeps in his own bed, attended by Charles. In the morning, four waiters serve a luxurious breakfast to Albert who also wears a waiter's uniform. The manager pleads with Albert to give up the charade, fearing for the reputation of the hotel, but Albert assures him it will be only a few more days. He tips the waiters and goes to work.

Albert draws a bath for Peter but refuses to polish Paul's shoes. Then, he refuses to walk the dogs, explaining that he is the personal servant to the Grand Duchess. He is ordered to Zenia's bedroom, where she orders him to walk the dogs; so, Albert summons Charles to bring his car. From the back seat of his convertible, Albert "walks" the four Russian wolfhounds, a Pomeranian, and a poodle through the park. Seeing Zenia and Peter on horseback in the park, Albert quickly gets out of the car and begins to walk the dogs properly. She orders him to return to the hotel to wash the dogs, and when next seen, Albert is shampooing a poodle in Peter's wash basin.

If Albert is having difficulty winning the affection of Zenia, he certainly is not without female companionship in the royal suite. Maxine, Zenia's maid, flirts with Albert and chides him for not paying attention to her. Albert sews Zenia's clothing while the Grand Duchess bathes in the next room, and upon noticing that it is the royal lingerie which he is mending, he kisses the delicate garment. Zenia then summons Albert to the bathroom, but she must call him three times before he can believe that he is being summoned to so private a place. He enters with both eyes shut, then he opens his eyes to see that she is standing to the side of the tub, wearing a dressing gown. He must fish her book from the tub.

Shortly after his departure from the bathroom, Maxine dries his coat sleeve as Albert complains that such tasks will drive him mad. Maxine explains that "a servant is not supposed to be a real man." "I understand," Albert answers. "Sexless like the angels." Maxine flirts with Albert once more, but the scene is interrupted by the entrance of Zenia. She administers more punishment for Albert by ordering him to sleep on the mat in front of her bedroom door. Albert laughs as he leaves the room for this punishment appeals to him.

That night, Zenia discovers that her money has doubled. She summons Albert to his sleeping place, and he arrives wearing a silk dressing gown. "I thought you'd like it," he says, as he primps before bed. She turns to him just as he is blowing a kiss in her direction. She leads him to his mat, and, as she enters the bedroom, she tells him she is nervous and sleeps with a loaded revolver. "If by accident this door should open during the night, you would be greeted by six bullets — not one of which would miss its mark." She sends him for a drink while she returns to counting her money. Albert brings a bottle of champagne with two glasses. She asks why there are two glasses, and he tells her they cannot both drink from one glass. She smashes his glass and says she could not imagine drinking with a waiter. Then she questions him about the money. Albert admits giving it to her, and she accuses him of being a blackmailer, spy, or thief and threatens to telephone the police. He calls the police for her, but she fails to report him. They kiss passionately: "With me it was love at first sight." "And I've loved you ever since you spilled the cream over me. It was fate."

The Grand Dukes enter and are shocked to see a Grand Duchess kissing a waiter, and such a bad waiter at that. Zenia quickly explains she was not serious and sends Albert from the room, then begins to cry. Peter rushes into the room with a newspaper and shows them a photograph of Albert with a horse. The caption reads that he is a millionaire turfman named Albert Belfort.

The next morning, impassioned by the kiss, Albert buys back Catherine the Great's necklace and reports to the royal suite without his uniform. He spots the newspaper and an envelope addressed to Albert Belfort. A note reads, "Albert — I am leaving Paris to start life anew. Thank you for trying to help us all. Can you forgive me? Zenia Pavlovna."

In the room below, Charles watches the chandelier swaying, but it is only the rumble of Albert exiting. Albert searches France for Zenia. Months pass, and it is the day of the races. The royal Russians are running an inn in the countryside. Paul says he would not be scrambling eggs if she had married Albert, but Zenia insists they have found their level and must make the best of the situation. Peter waits tables and brings a glass of wine to Albert at his car. They recognize each other, and Albert enters the inn. Zenia races out the back door to the garden, and Albert follows. There, they embrace, while the rest of the royal entourage dances with joy for all their good fortune.

The film is not technically innovative but produced with care and a substantial budget. Relating a romance of fashionable people in a witty manner, it is a prime example of the society comedy film of the mid-1920's. The story is lighthearted, not surprising or instructive, but it is told with expert pacing and style.

ANTHONY SLIDE
Seventh Heaven

Review reprinted from Frank N. Magill, Magill's Survey of Cinema: *Silent Films (Salem Press, 1982).*

Released: 1927
Production: William Fox
Direction: Frank Borzage (AA)
Screenplay: Benjamin Glazer (AA); based on the play *Seventh Heaven* by Austin Strong
Titles: Katherine Hilliker and H.H. Caldwell
Cinematography: Ernest Palmer
Editing: Katherine Hilliker and H.H. Caldwell
Music: Erno Rapee and Lew Pollack
Length: 9 reels/8,500 feet

Principal characters:	
Diane	Janet Gaynor
Chico	Charles Farrell
Colonel Brissac	Ben Bard
Gobin	David Butler
Madame Gobin	Marie Mosquini
Papa Boul	Albert Gran
Nana	Gladys Brockwell
Father Chevillon	Emile Chautard

It is probably no overstatement to describe Frank Borzage as the screen's greatest romantic director. Critic Andrew Sarris has hailed Borzage as "that rarity of rarities, an uncompromising romanticist." So many of the director's films show the romantic side of existence, usually in an atmosphere or environment that is heavy with poverty and suffering. Borzage's best romantic works are *Street Angel* (1928), *The River* (1929), *Liliom* (1930), *A Farewell to Arms* (1932), and *Man's Castle* (1933). These films all propagandize a theory, which is stated in one of the titles in another Borzage great romantic creation, *7th Heaven*: "For those who will climb it, there is a ladder leading from the depths to the heights — from the sewer to the stars — the ladder of courage."

Borzage (1893-1962) began his film career as an actor in the early teens. He became a director — first of his own films — in 1916, and soon became one of the industry's top directors, working for all the major studios. He joined the William Fox Company in 1926 and was to remain there, as probably its highest paid director, until 1932. Although he continued to direct until 1959, the pinnacle of Borzage's success was undoubtedly the years with Fox, and his finest achievement with that studio was *7th Heaven.*

7th Heaven was one of the last great silent films, produced in the year that also saw the release of *The Jazz Singer*, and, like a number of other Fox films from this period, it was generally released with a musical score recorded, sound-on-film, by the Fox Movietone system. In fact, when *7th Heaven* received its New York premiere, on May 25, 1927, it was preceded by a number of sound Movietone shorts featuring the likes of Raquel Meller and Gertrude Lawrence. The music score, composed by Erno Rapee and Lew Pollack, is an integral part of the film, and disproves the theory that silent films may be enjoyed in silence. Not only does it include its famous, and still popular, theme song, "Diane," but also, as Diane and Chico declare their love for each other, a soprano is heard singing "Oh Divine Redeemer" by Gounod, and there is nothing at all incongruous in this. The singing adds to the emotional intensity of the scenes. Similarly, a few moments later, as the couple learns of the outbreak of World War I, rousing martial music breaks into the soft love-tones of the score, interrupting the melodic score just as World War I will interrupt the young lover's lives together.

In the film, Chico (Charles Farrell) works in the sewers of Paris — he is first seen standing in the sewers looking out through a manhole cover which lets in the sunlight — but he dreams of one day becoming a street cleaner. As he describes himself, he is "a remarkable fellow." Diane (Janet Gaynor) is a poor waif, living in a slum with her vicious sister, Nana (played with superb cruelty by Gladys Brockwell). When an aunt and uncle arrive, who might take Diane out of the slums, she is unable to lie when they question her concerning her morality, and so she is left to live out her sordid existence with Nana. Diane is chased into the streets by the whip-carrying Nana, but Chico intervenes and threatens to throw Nana down the manhole into the sewer unless she leaves Diane alone.

As Chico, ignoring Diana, sits in the gutter and eats his meal, Father Chevillon (Emile Chautard) appears. Chico tells the Father that he does not believe in God; he had tested him twice, but God had failed him. In addition, Chico claims God owes him ten francs for the candles that he purchased when he prayed to be made a street cleaner and to be given a wife. In response, the Father gives Chico two medallions and a chit which will get him the sought-after job of street cleaner.

After the priest has left, Diane is about to leave, but the police arrive on the scene and are about to arrest the girl for prostitution until Chico says that she is his wife. Because the police will check Chico's address and see if he is really telling the truth, Chico is forced to take Diane back to his lodging, which is on the top, seventh floor, of the building. In a scene of brilliant technical ingenuity, the pair slowly climb from the street and its sewers to Chico's apartment and heaven. The apartment symbolizes Chico's outlook on life, "Never look down. Always look up." (Strangely enough, the stairs which rise straight up in the opening reels of film have suddenly become spiral for the film's close.) The couple's relationship — and at this point it is not even that — is a purely platonic one. Diane peers, from under the bedclothes of the bed she will occupy alone, at Chico, stripped to the waist and bathing himself.

Chico's outlook on life becomes even sunnier once he has become a street cleaner, and is working with his new friend Gobin (played by director-to-be David Butler), who lives with his wife in an apartment across the rooftops from Chico. Through simple episodes, such as Diane cutting Chico's hair, a loving relationship develops between the young couple. Diane tells Chico that "God brought me to you." Unable to express his love for Diane in words, Chico brings her a white wedding dress. He says the three words that symbolize their relationship, "Chico. Diane. Heaven." (In fact, lip-readers will note that the couple is speaking in French during the film's close-ups, and, actually, recite, "Chico. Diane. Ciel.") Chico teaches Diane courage, and she tells him she will never be afraid again.

At this point, the war intervenes, and Chico is ordered to mobilize. He decides to give God a chance by performing a marriage ceremony between the two of them, with the medallions given to him by Father Chevillon serving to sanctify their marriage vows. Chico tells Diane that each morning at eleven, the two will renew their vows with the words "Diane. Chico. Heaven," and the two will be spiritually joined together. Shortly after Chico's departure, Diane's sister Nana reappears to try and re-assert her dominance over the girl, but, thanks to Chico, Diane is no longer afraid and this time it is Diane who takes a whip and drives Nana from the apartment.

While Chico is fighting at the front, Diane gets a job in an armaments factory, where she rejects the affectionate attentions of Colonel Brissac (Ben Bard); and each morning at eleven Diane and Chico come together through their overwhelming love for each other. Diane is in Paris, Chico is at the front, but they "are shoulder to shoulder — that is all that matters."

One incident of World War I is featured in *7th Heaven*, and that is General Galliene's marshaling of some one thousand Parisian taxicabs to rush troops of the 62nd Division twenty-five miles to the battlefront to prevent the German advance on the city. One of Diane and Chico's friends, Papa Boule (Albert Gran), drives his taxi, Eloise, to the front, where it is blown up leaving the tearful cabby with nothing but the horn as a memento to the taxicab's bravery. The special effects for the war scenes were created by Louis Witte and were filmed, as were all the street scenes, at the new Fox studios at what was then called Movietone City and is now called Century City in Los Angeles.

As the war ends, the audience quite clearly sees Chico killed. Father Chevillon visits Diane with the news, bringing Chico's medallion with him. First Diane will not believe him, pointing out that every morning at eleven she communed with Chico, but as she realizes the truth, she turns her anger on the priest, striking him across the chest and crying. "For four years I called this Heaven — I prayed — I believed in God — I believed he would bring Chico back to me." Suddenly, there is a sharp cut to the crowds outside celebrating the armistice, and in the midst of the crowd, Chico is seen, blinded but struggling to return to Heaven and to Diane. As he mounts the stairs, it is eleven o'clock and the two lovers call out to each other. "They thought I was dead, but I'll never die," says Chico, and, as the two embrace, a flood of sunlight pours in through the window. Love has conquered all, even death. It is an extraordinary ending, so heavy with emotion and spirituality that it totally overwhelms the audience and enables us to suspend all disbelief.

7th Heaven created a new romantic film team with Charles Farrell and Janet Gaynor, and for several more years, the two were to delight audiences in light comedy-dramas (often with interpolated musical numbers), such as *Christina* (1920), *Sunny Side Up* (1929), *Lucky Star* (1929), and *Delicious* (1931). Only the film *Street Angel*, however, approached the emotional intensity of *7th Heaven*, and that was also directed, a year later, by Borzage.

The film was as much of a critical success as the original stageplay, with Helen Menken, had been in 1922. *Photoplay* (July, 1927) commented,

> One John Golden play plus one talented director plus two brilliant young people equals one fine picture. . . . It is permeated with the spirit of youth, of young love, of whimsy. . . .
> It's tender and tragic and wholly appealing, splashed now and then with that grandly human comedy for which Director Frank Borzage is known.

In *The Film Spectator* (May 28, 1927), Welford Beaton wrote, "It's the soul of *7th Heaven* that gets you, the soul put into it by an understanding script, sympathetic direction and superb acting."

The film industry agreed with its critics, and at the first Academy Awards ceremony on May 6, 1929, *7th Heaven* was honored with three awards: Best Actress to Janet Gaynor, Best Direction to Frank Borzage, and Best Writing (adaptation) to Benjamin Glazer. In addition, *7th Heaven* was nominated for Best Picture and Best Art Direction.

In 1937, *7th Heaven* was remade, under the direction of Henry King, and starred James Stewart and Simone Simon. Neither artistically nor commercially did it match the success of its silent predecessor.

MOLLY HASKELL
Sunrise

Extract from "Sunrise" a review article in Film Comment, *Summer 1971.*

1927, Fox Film Corporation, 95 minutes.
Director: F.W. Murnau
Screenplay: Carl Mayer
From the short story "A Trip to Tilsit" by Herman Suderman
Photography: Charles Rosher and Karl Struss
Art Director: Rochus Gliese

Cast
The Man (Ansass) . . . . George O'Brien
The Wife (Indre) . . . . Janet Gaynor
The Woman from the City . . . . Margaret Livingstone
The Maid . . . . Bodil Rising
The Barber . . . . Ralph Sipperly
The Manicure Girl . . . . Jane Winton
The Obtrusive Gentleman . . . . Arthur Houseman
The Obliging Gentleman . . . . Eddie Boland

Among other things, *Sunrise* is about a man losing — and regaining — his mind. The oppositions in *Sunrise* (and it is dialectical on every level) are between sunrise and sunset, the country and the city, good and evil, salvation and sin, divine grace and black magic, natural and unnatural acts, and finally the blonde, beatific wife (Janet Gaynor) and the dark, sultry city woman (Margaret Livingstone) in their struggle for The Man's soul.

It is through the visualization of mental images that 1) temptation is represented — in the swinging, night-light world the city woman conjures up; 2) the possibility of murder is posed — in the image of the drowning of the wife; 3) loss of mental control is indicated — the husband's drifting on water; and finally 4) sanity is restored — when husband and wife walk hand in hand across the congested traffic circle which is transformed, in the ultimate solipsism of superimposition, into a leafy bower. Thus the victory of mind over matter, love over evil, magic over logic, and film over reality.

The film opens with a Bauhaus-style collage of graphics, illustrating the city in summer, a train station, posters picturing seaside vacations, dissolving eventually into "three-dimensional" reality as the vacationers emigrate to the country. The image of the city balances the agitation of its angled, industrial architecture with a kind of excitement, and emerges more or less neutral at this stage. The values of the city, counterposed to those of the country, will change perceptibly according to the point of view. When the city woman depicts its pleasures to the husband, the images are violent, cacaphonic and sexual. The rhythm is pulsating, overpowering. It can almost be heard. (No telephone has ever rung so deafeningly as the one in *Dr. Mabuse, Der Spieler* which jiggles up and down.) Indeed, Murnau's city often seems like a metaphor for the sound film, trying to burst into the peaceful haven of the country, the silent film.

When the man and wife alight after the transitional streetcar ride, the city is at first threatening and dangerous and then, after their reconciliation, submissive. The amusement park is something else again — a place where anything can happen (a pig can get drunk), and whose rhythm is represented in a dizzying repetition of circular motifs. The theory that the fair (as in *Caligari*) and the circle (the revolving door in *The Last Laugh*) represent, on the one hand, a regression to childhood, and, on the other, anarchy and chaos would apply here, but without the negative implications. The amusements are a deserved regression, a momentary abandonment after the tension of estrangement and the solemnity of the reunion.

As the city is crowded, congested, sophisticated and splintered, the country is simple, wholesome, a community both physically and mystically. Not only the people but even the animals unite against the city woman's enchantment of the husband. When he returns from his rendezvous carrying the bullrushes she has given him (to save himself in the drowning), a horse nuzzles him violently. The wife is seen the next morning, surrounded by and feeding the chickens. In an astonishing example of *clairsentience*, their dog dashes to the boat in an agitated effort to stop his mistress from going. And finally, as the row toward the middle of the lake, the sound of the church bells recede in the distance and a flock of birds resting on the river quickly disperses.

There is no doubt that the spell of the city woman, who stalks the night and disappears with daylight, is supernatural. (It must be remembered that, in *Nosferatu*, Murnau made one of the earliest vampire films.) She has only to whistle softly outside the husband's window, and he is galvanized. He dresses hurriedly, rushes to a designated meeting place. The camera follows him and suddenly, in a gloriously unexpected camera movement, takes a shortcut through the bushes, arriving first, to behold the city woman waiting, her profile silhouetted against the moon. The man does not embrace but rather succumbs — violently — to her. She takes the initiative, cradling him in her arms, and outlining her plan. When he returns to his cottage, he is like a man drugged, heavy, moving in a kind of stupor, as if his blood had been drained. He sleeps fitfully, "drowning" symbolically in the water in which he intends to throw his wife. The following day, rowing his wife to the middle of the river, he is still under the spell. When he rises to kill her, he becomes a virtual monster — deranged, wooden, his eyes dull and his body towering over her. She clasps her hands in prayer. At this, he recoils — like the vampire in *Nosferatu* when confronted with a cross. He covers his face with his hands and the chimes ring victoriously. The moment of danger is passed; she is saved but still terrified. When they reach the shore, she races up the hill, falling twice, and climbs aboard the trolley. Racing after her, he barely makes it aboard, whereupon they — and we — are swept into one of the most ecstatic movements in all of cinema. The psychological suspension between anguish and relief is exquisitely, and physically, sustained by the breathtakingly lyrical, delirious motion of the trolley through real space. By a combination of different camera set-ups extended through gliding motion, the sense of weightlessness is perpetuated and the sphere expands to include normal life which (in the form of the conductor and then a cyclist alongside the trolley) gradually resumes, providing a relief and preparing for the moment when they will "hit bottom" in the midst of the city. They have been brought together, physically if not spiritually, in a suspended state of temporary grace.

Nothing ever quite equals that one matchless, magic passage — as, perhaps, the pleasure of fulfillment can never equal the exquisite anguish of anticipation— but the rest of the film does contain its share of tender moments and a deepening through repetition. The progression towards forgiveness and atonement is Christian. He offers her food (communion) which she accepts; she breaks down, achieving a release; he gives her flowers; she still can't face him. With the ringing of the chimes — the one link, besides the trolley, between city and country — she looks at him, and it is then they enact, by proxy, the ceremony of marriage, thus resanctifying their own.

The return to the country retraces the first part of the film, but with the husband wanting to save his wife rather than drown her, thereby undoing the spell through action, and expiating his sin. The final act of redemption is performed by the wife, since it is the discovery of her body, or the cry announcing it, that keeps the husband from strangling the city woman. The ultimate victory of goodness is that it is infinite.

Murnau makes full use of the expressionistic vocabulary: a raked dining table in the home of the peasants where the city woman is staying, emphasizing their poverty and precariousness next to her; lighting which gives the wife an iridescent halo and surrounds the city woman in a miasmal mist. But it is in the camera, rather than in the characters or sets, that awareness resides, and in which the process of discovery is initiated. The camera's orientation is neither that of any one character nor is it totally objective, in the manner of the omniscient third-person narrator. It is curious, even eccentric, suddenly taking off on its own, and arriving, as in the shortcut, at something worth discovering. There is another instance shortly afterward. The city woman, having persuaded the husband to murder his wife, disappears. The camera suddenly focuses on the ground, where footsteps can be discerned. In an unusually long movement it follows the footsteps to a clearing where the city woman is standing, a bunch of bullrushes in hands. The effect of such surprise is to keep the spectator off guard, in a mild state of suspense. It also prevents the movie from being too rigidly formal, or academically classical. In *Sunrise* Murnau breathes life into an archetypal arrangement, and he raises the archetypal to a definitive expression of poetic cinema.

GILBERT SELDES
The Crowd

"A Fine American Movie" [The Crowd] *a review in the New Republic, March 7, 1928.*

In the long time that has passed since King Vidor directed "The Big Parade," he has done, I believe, some small pictures; his heart and his mind have been in "The Crowd," a picture originally released on the regular programs, not advertised as a super-feature, and to me the most interesting development in the American movie in years. (After a week at the Capitol, it has been put on as a special at the Astor.)

It is not entirely a fine picture; either Mr. Vidor or his collaborator, Mr. John V.A. Weaver, has given it scenes which are feeble or vulgar, and he has fumbled the handling of emotions in an attempt to get a laugh. Yet negatively the picture is extremely important because it breaks completely with the stereotype of the feature film. There is virtually no plot; there is no exploitation of sex in the love interest; there is no physical climax, no fight, no scheduled thrill. The characters, all commonplace people, act singularly unlike moving picture characters and singularly like human beings; there is no villain, no villainy, no success. "The Crowd" is absorbingly interesting, at moments charged with tremendous emotional excitement, exceptionally intelligent and satisfactory.

It condenses a few years in the life of a boy who comes to New York persuaded that he will get somewhere, do big things, be somebody, if he ever gets an opportunity. He becomes one of a hundred clerks in an insurance office; with thousands of others he kisses a girl at Coney Island; even his marriage does not isolate him, and the birth of his first child brings him to a maternity ward where hundreds of beds are aligned .He gets a raise of eight dollars a week, his second child is killed, he gives up his job, he can't succeed at any other, his wife starts to leave him but cannot carry it through, they go to the theater together, and as they rock and roar with laughter they are again submerged in a crowd which also rocks and roars.

In the movie sense, this is no plot; the absence of romance in the treatment is equally unlike the movies. But it is Mr. Vidor's triumph that he can make precisely this absence of romance seem actually tender and beautiful. The boy goes out, while his wife's family waits for Christmas dinner, to borrow some gin; he gets drunk and returns only after all have gone except his wife, who is in bed. The tradition, the romantic tradition of the movies, demands here a scene; Mr. Vidor gives the wife a smile of sympathy, the husband a moment of contrition, and the scene ends with them quarreling lightly over the propriety of her raising the umbrella which is one of his presents to her. When the child is run down by a motor truck, the father, driven mad by the city noises which he thinks are preventing the baby's return to consciousness, rushes into the street beseeching passers-by, motorists, fire engines, crowds, to be quiet; almost mad with the noise of the crowd, he returns to the room; the doctor has meanwhile removed his instrument from the child's heart; the father learns the news from the mother's face. So in everything fine in the picture, the treatment is fresh, credible, creative of intense emotion.

It is clear that, to make these things fresh and moving, the technique must be out of the ordinary. It is. But before coming to that, I must indicate Mr. Vidor's two errors. When the boy and girl are married, they go to Niagara Falls, and there is a long sequence of pictures on the sleeper. I have never thought jokes about the bridal night funny in themselves, and Mr. Vidor has worked the old ones to death; the taste is quite bad here, the gags are tedious. The purpose was to give Mr. Vidor a scene on a knoll, with the falls as background, where the desire of the boy and girl manifests itself the next day. It was a good scene, but the business in the sleeper was romantic in the tawdriest way, a serious blemish.

The second fault baffles me to explain. Possibly Mr. Weaver, having once written a bit of verse about a Victrola, thinks that instrument really the machine out of which the god of drama springs; possibly Mr. Vidor, perplexed about his ending, took the easiest way. The wife has left the house; she returns on a pretext and the husband, who has got a job that day, asks her to go to the theater with him, and gives her some flowers. Their reconciliation is barely begun; they hardly know how to go about it. And so a talking machine, which has not appeared before, is started by the husband; they dance to "There's Everything Nice About You," the child joins them in laughter, and this scene dissolves into them laughing at the vaudeville show which ends the picture. Did Mr. Vidor mean to suggest that even in the expression of their deepest emotions they have to call on a standardized mechanical aid? It is the most flattering explanation, but if it is true it points to another defect — lack of preparation, lack of significant emphasis. As the picture stands, it looks more as if Mr. Vidor himself had to call in mechanics.

And of mechanics he is a master. Here is a man who knows how to take moving pictures — an excessively rare thing in the moving picture industry. He takes them so that they have movement, so that they have beauty, and, rarest of all, so that they have meaning. A little boy comes up a flight of stairs to discover what has happened to his father: the stairs, the walls, the ceiling, form a long tapering rectangular box through which we look upon the little figure; by the time he is three-quarters of the way up, the father has died for us, although we have seen nothing of him, and Mr. Vidor breaks the movement by having another figure come down to meet the boy. The grown lad comes to New York on a ferry; we are not limited to his view of the city; we see what the city *means* to him, from his early confusion, his bewilderment at regular blocks of buildings, its speed, its carelessness, its unapprehended rhythm. Then the city engulfs him. The camera sweeps the city, picks out a building, miraculously describes all its majesty, beauty, and aloofness. A shot is taken so that the tier after tier of window and stonework lies flat before us, slowly it rises like a painted cardboard wall pushed from behind; we approach the pinnacle breathlessly, the building absorbs us physically, leans over, takes us in, and when it is righted the camera begins to pick out a floor, a series of windows on that floor, a separate window, and we are inside, on an anonymous floor, of an anonymous company, and our hero — ourself — sits at one of a hundred desks.

Mr. Vidor has avoided the complete stylization of the crowd — the method of "Metropolis." Endless doors open and endless crowds come to endlessly moving elevators; but there is no machine-like precision. It is to me poignant enough — that people in their own way still do the same things .So the different crowds have varying rhythms and pace, are friendly or menacing or indifferent. They have not only their own meaning, but their function in the picture.

James Murray, who plays the boy, is a genuine find — the story of his siege of Hollywood is highly romantic and absolutely true; he reminds me of the young Charles Ray, and is beautifully suited to Mr. Vidor's quiet method of expression. The great player of the film is, however, not the lead but Eleanor Boardman, who plays the girl. Except for a few moments when she imitated the Mae Marsh of years ago, everything in her creation was personal, worked out from within, and terribly affecting. She brought me close to tears more than once; she satisfied my inner sense of the decorum and rightness of methods all the time. She grew up in the brief hour of the movie from a cheap little girl to a suffering and tender woman, with weaknesses and powers. It is altogether a beautiful performance.

"The Crowd" does not follow precisely the outline Mr. Vidor gave to me about a year ago, when it was almost finished. I should like to think that the one really bad spot was not left in at his order, and that his neutral ending — the boy getting back his original job — was not omitted at the command of his employers. Whatever the truth may be, the Metro-Goldwyn-Mayer corporation is to be congratulated on having Mr. Vidor and on giving him his head, and he is to be congratulated on courage and intelligence and the mastery of his art. His future is bound to be interesting; what remains to see is whether he can achieve greater freedom in production, and get material even more amenable to his powerful and delicate hands.

The Wind

JOHN TIBBETTS
The Wind

"*Extract from Vital Geography: Victor Seastrom's* The Wind,"
Literature/Film Quarterly, *Vol. 1, No. 3, July 1973.*

When Letty Mason (Lillian Gish) arrives at a whistle-stop town
in the middle of a vast, windy desert, she exclaims, "My, this wind
is awful isn't it? I wish it would stop." At once we meet the two
antagonists. Letty and the desert wind square off immediately with
her opening statement; the struggle begins. Antagonists they stay
until the end of the film. In another five minutes are introduced
to the secondary characters, Lige Hightower, the cowboy (portrayed by Lars Hanson, a favorite actor used many times by Seastrom in Sweden) and the "city man," Wirt (Montague Love). Wirt,
incidentally is one more in that series of movie rascals in the
Twenties who swooped in from the decadent city to lure winsome
heroines into moral ruin — another prime example being Lennox
Sanderson in Griffith's *Way Down East.*

Letty has come to live with a cousin and his wife and children.
After a brief stay she is forced to look elsewhere for shelter because
her cousin's wife grows jealous of her, imagining some sort of
liaison between Letty and her husband. Letty's search for shelter
forces her hand, and she accepts the proposal of the cowboy Lige.
The marriage is a loveless one. Because of her frigidity their relations
grow worse and the wind grows stronger, as Letty's delicate sensi-
bilities begin to erode. Enter Wirt, whom Lige has found injured
from a fall and has brought to the house to convalesce. While Wirt
is there a terrific storm comes up. and he and Lige leave to recapture
some strayed cattle. Wirt secretly returns and in a night of violence
assaults Letty. She shoots him and tries to bury him beneath the
blowing sands. When the wind persists in uncovering the body, she
goes mad.

Nothing less than the invisible wind is made animate and tangible throughout. Every device possible is employed to provide this
effect; there are visual metaphors, wherein the wind is personified
first as a wild animal, then as Letty herself, and finally as her guilt.
The wind is further defined through its function, in its effects on
things and people. And finally it is visualized through camera
technique and frame displacement.

Use of the visual metaphor occurs throughout. An early title likens the wind to a great, careering stallion, and we see a series of ghostly double exposures of a fiery white horse rearing through the clouds. Later this symbol of wild and free fury, this near anthropomorphic treatment of an elemental force, is extended to Letty herself, as when the burning image is superimposed over her face in the climactic moments of the film. This metaphoric treatment of a horse galloping through the heavens is incomparably superior to a similar effect in Ingram's *Four Horsemen of the Apocalypse*. Under Seastrom's hands the image seems to burn as if it were shot in negative; the coordinated fury of its galloping seems caught in slow motion.

The introductory shots of the train arriving at night seem to give form to the wind. The blowing white dust defines the silhouette of the train with tunnel shapes of cloud, just as the characters are continually surrounded by rough mantles of blowing dust. In many other ways is the wind intensely visual. It is felt by its function. In this way it is present at all times, even when the action is inside. When Letty brushes dust off the wedding bed, we feel at once not only the pervading presence of the wind, but also recognize an effective symbol for the sterility of her marriage with Lige. The total permeation of the element into her life is implied.

In the climactic scenes the implied presence of the wind is most effectively felt, not only through its effects on material objects, but through a masterful treatment of the camera and the frame. Wirt's return to the house and his attack on Letty seem to unhinge the whole frame from its supports. The entire frame seethes and sways. The single slatted lamp sways in the darkness, the striped shadows crawling over Letty's huddled form. We seem to float in a series of dizzying arcs; her form slowly appears at the corner of the titled frame, then moves away as if floating aimlessly in a vortex. All anchors are loosed; there is only a kind of freefall, of vertigo. We are one with Letty, and for us, as well as for her, the wind has swept away all supports of gravity; we exist in a silent and slow vacuum. As if by accident, fluid and offhand camera movement catches her swaying form as well as the movement of the lamp and the shadows, conveying the final shattering control the wind exercises over her. Complete fantasy takes over and the interior seems to crumple and break up before our eyes, as if shaken apart by some vast supernatural agent. The sequence culminates in a series of dissolves of the interior and her swaying form to fantastic slow-motion shots of the aforementioned galloping stallion. Everything has led to this final unification of her mind with the elemental force of the wind. It is a striking metamorphosis.

In superb contrast to the fury that went before it, the mute eloquence of the following sequence conveys a cold kind of madness. It is morning after Wirt's vicious assault and Letty's final breakdown. The first shot is a high-angle dolly moving in and down upon the back of her head to a holstered pistol lying in dust on the table. The dust, our inability to see her face, her motionlessness, the pointed observation of the camera, overwhelm us with its cumulative suggestive power. The complete silence and quiet of the scene provide one last respite before the wind's final bow, as it were, when all suggestion and metaphor are dropped and the wind, like a master thief in a melodrama, doffs its disguises and strides to center stage toward the denouement.

This is of course the most famous scene in the film, when Letty's attempts to bury Wirt's body are thwarted by the wind. Her back to us, we see the shovel lifting and falling past her shoulder, the sand and dusting arching up from it in little spurts. Then we see her face pressed against the window pane watching in stupefaction as the blowing wind slowly reveals Wirt's face underneath a layer of sand. It's as if Wirt were partially submerged in a running sea, as if something has ascended from the depths of a nightmare and were taking form before us. The wind, through magnificent indifference (or in moral judgment) to Letty, reveals her deed. The wind seems human, to act with a purpose, to have knowledge we don't, to use that knowledge to both reveal and destroy. We are enlightened while Letty goes mad. At the same time the wind represents her inability to escape her act, that moment in all our lives when fears long submerged begin to take familiar shape again. Seastrom's treatment of the wind has proceeded inexorably from the opening visual metaphor of the stallion, to the linking of that stallion with Letty in the aforementioned series of dissolves, and to the final identification of it with her conscience. That the wind has assumed this moralistic role along with its other motivational and identifying ones — that it is now a cathartic element in Letty's mind — represents the film's peak achievement.

As I pointed out earlier, nature has become not only the geographical location that surrounds her, but the dramatic and transforming element of the narrative. In this way it is fully Seastrom's work, linking indirectly with the earlier *Outlaw and His Wife*. Although the tacked-on ending at first seems ludicrous, it *does* fulfill the Catheresque idea that acceptance means sanity and life. Letty's frigidity was a brittle kind of barrier like her defiance of the wind.

The wind's revelation of Wirt's buried body breaks that symbolic resistance. One might fancifully imagine a cold blast churning its way through her, or a white light dispelling an attic's shadows and cobwebs. When Lige returns, he calms her and they stand together in the doorway facing into the wind. It whips her hair back and billows her skirts. As it plays about her, molding the skirts to her slim body, we experience the light-headed feeling that a nightmare has recently been exorcised. It is not the same wind that evoked Letty's opening exclamation; it gently enfolds her body now; it is almost as if through her own transformation it, too, were subtly changed. It is one of the strangest victories in cinema.

Sometimes the farthest vistas of nature tell us something about the neighbor next door. When an artist reveals the participation and interaction of man and nature, he deals with an ever-changing aspect. So, too, is the wind an ambiguous presence, its lineaments ever changing as it moves over and defines form. It is capable of all shapes, just as truth finds its many expressions.

TOM MILNE
Show People

From an article "Davies" in Sight and Sound, *Vol. 37 No. 4, Autumn 1968, pages 200-201.*

Two years ago at a Venice Festival retrospective, I saw my first Marion Davies film — it was either *Show People* or *The Patsy* — and was duly astonished. Could this enchanting comedienne, who cheerfully sent up everybody from Lillian Gish and Gloria Swanson to Marion Davies herself, possibly be the model for Susan Alexander, that archetypal product of the casting-couch for whom Citizen Kane so desperately tried to buy stardom as an opera singer? Well, she could and she couldn't. In his autobiography, King Vidor has described the birth-pangs of *Show People*, shedding a good deal of light on her problematic career. The film was to be a burlesque, more or less, of Gloria Swanson's rise from the slapstick ranks of Mack Sennett bathing beauties to enthronement as a dramatic actress and as the Marquise de la Falaise de la Coudray. A key scene would have Peggy Pepper, aspiring Southern belle soon to be metamorphosed into Patricia Pepoire, turn up for her first day at the studio bent on wringing more tears with her histrionics than both Gishes put together, and instead receive a custard pie slap in the face. Marion Davies loved the idea. William Randolph Hearst, unfortunately, objected to the indignity to be inflicted on his beloved, and Mr. Hearst's word was law. So Peggy Pepper is sprayed, equally effectively but apparently more classily, with a soda siphon.

No doubt Hearst was bewitched by that demure china doll face with its appealing blue eyes and halo of golden hair (but how could he have missed the mischievous grin and that upper lip which could curl into the most devastating Brer Rabbit parody of the rosebud pout which was all the rage?). At any rate, for several years after they met in 1917 when she was a chorus girl in New York and he a multi-millionaire tycoon and newspaper proprietor, he spent a fortune financing her pictures and promoting them in his papers in an attempt to buy her stardom as a winsome young romantic maiden. From her 1918 debut in *Runaway Romany*, through fifteen or sixteen pictures to 1922, she appears to have had only one real box-office success, as Mary Tudor in *When Knighthood was in Flower*, the film which did finally establish her as a star. Meanwhile, the sweet young maiden longed to play hardboiled blondes and comedy.

As prints of so few of these early films have survived, it is difficult to say whether critics and public were right in cold-shouldering Hearst's creation. The most one can say is that in *The Belle of New York* (1919), where she tinkled tambourines and dispensed forgiveness with the best of them as a Salvation Army lass saving souls amid the squalor of the New York beer parlours, she is the only thing worth watching in a creaky melodrama: her exquisite beauty shines through soulfully, and she acts with a restraint and repose rare at the time.

Gradually, however, things changed. By 1927, she was fast earning a new reputation as a comedienne with *The Red Mill* (directed by Roscoe Arbuckle under his pseudonym of William Goodrich: one up to Hearst for employing him after the scandal), *Tillie the Toiler, The Fair Co-Ed* and *Quality Street*. And 1928 was the *annus mirabilis* which matched her talent for the first time with a director — King Vidor — who obviously understood it and could use it to the full. In *The Patsy*, a warm and deliciously funny Cinderella story in which she gets the better of her spoiled elder sister by emerging outrageously as a fully-fledged flapper, she proves that she could snap her garters as gaily as Clara Bow and do fearsomely exact parodies of Gish, Mae Murray and Pola Negri. In *Show People*, she mercilessly flays the pretensions of Hollywood glamour queens with languorous poses in love scenes opposite an effete and greasy leading man, and wavering attempts to keep her nose from twitching as her lip curls to the regulation cupid's bow sneer; she cheerfully mocks America's sweetheart with her frolicsome entry in sunbonnet, ringlets and frilly print dress to make a coy display of her dramatic abilities to a startled clerk in the casting office; and she reveals that she was second not even to Gloria Swanson in her mastery of slapstick, or Beatrice Lillie in her gift for innuendo by raised eyebrow. The screen test sequence, in which she subtly mismanages all her emotions and expressions, sub-vocalises like mad when given a letter supposedly containing news of her stricken lover, and — after barely managing to produce a furrowed forehead for the heartbreak — dissolves into floods of tears for the comedy bit, is a superb example of comic timing.

Doubtless it was Hearst's influence which turned *Show People* into Who's Who at M-G-M, with Chaplin making a charming unbilled appearance as an autograph-hunting Charlie, John Gilbert turning up to be briefly adored; Lew Cody and Elinor Glyn sauntering by, and Douglas Fairbanks, William S. Hart and George K.

Arthur clowning in the commissary. Doubtless it was King Vidor who turned it into what is now a fascinating documentary on Hollywood studio methods, with detailed backstage scenes, intriguing glimpses of the shooting of a slapstick chase, amiable satire on the star system (the leading man's shuddering with revulsion as he is splashed with a bucket of water after supposedly diving to the rescue in a lake) and many in-jokes (Vidor's own *Bardelys the Magnificent* is the 'art film' which Peggy Pepper drools over, and on which slapstick star Billy Boone pours so much scorn). But the engaging, offbeat charm belongs to Marion Davies alone.

Show People

Appendices

Appendix A
Cross Section of Studio Activity, 1925

From page 90, *Photoplay,*January 1925, "What the Stars and Directors Are Doing NOW," here is a selection of some names and places and titles that may evoke connections for readers of these volumes on "American Movies: The First Thirty Years."

WEST COAST. Buster Keaton Studio, 1025 Lillian Way: Buster Keaton directing himself in *Seven Chances*.

Charles Chaplin Studio, 1416 La Brea Ave, inactive.

FBO Studio, Melrose and Gower Sts: Gothic Productions, Tod Browning directing *Silk Stocking Sal*, with Evelyn Brent. . . . B.P. Schulberg Productions, Louis Gasnier completes *White Man* with Alice Joyce. Production soon to begin on *Capital Punishment* with Clara Bow and Owen Moore. . . . Larry Semon Productions, Larry Semon directing himself in *The Wizard of Oz*.

Fox Studio, 1401 N. Western Ave: George Marshall directing the "Van Bibber's" series. Lynn Reynolds directing *Riders of the Purple Sage* with Tom Mix.

First National Productions, United Studios: Ritz-Carlton Productions, Joseph Henabery directing *The Scarlet Power* [*Cobra*] with Rudolph Valentino and Nita Naldi.

Hollywood Studios, 6642 Santa Monica Blvd: Harold Lloyd Productions, untitled comedy with Jobyna Ralston.

Ince Studio, Culver City: Thomas H. Ince Productions, James Horne directing *The Desert Fiddler* with Charles Ray, Betty Blythe.

Lasky Studio, 1520 Vine St: Paul Bern directing *Tomorrow's Love*, with Agnes Ayres. . . Clarence Badger directing *New Wives for Old* with Betty Compson. . . Raoul Walsh directing *East of Suez* with Pola Negri, Edmund Lowe. . . Alan Crosland directing *Contraband* with Lois Wilson, Noah Beery.

Metro-Goldwyn-Mayer Studio, Culver City: Erich Von Stroheim directing *The Merry Widow* with Mae Murray, John Gilbert. . . Rupert Hughes directing *Excuse Me* with Conrad Nagel, Norma Shearer. . . Victor Seastrom directing *Kings in Exile.*

Pickford-Fairbanks Studio, 7100 Santa Monica Blvd,inactive.

Hal Roach Studios, Culver City: Arthur Stone in an untitled comedy. . . The Gang in an untitled comedy.

Universal Studio, Universal City: Rupert Julian directing *The Phantom of the Opera* with Lon Chaney, Mary Philbin, Norman Kerry . . . King Baggott directing *Raffles.*

Vitagraph Studio, 1708 Talmadge St: J. Stuart Blackton directing *The Redeeming Sin* with Nazimova, Lou Tellegen.

Warner Bros Studio, 5842 Sunset Blvd: Mal St. Clair directing *Thin Ice* with Tom Moore

EAST COAST. Biograph Studio, 807 East 175th St: *The One Way Street* with Anna Q. Nilsson and Ben Lyon.

Paramount Studio, Pierce Ave and Sixth St, Long Island City: Frank Tuttle directing *Miss Bluebeard* with Bebe Daniels, Raymond Griffith. . . Dimitri Buchowetzki directing *The Swan* with Frances Howard, Adolphe Menjou.

Tec-Art Studio, 318 East 48th St: Inspiration Pictures, John Robertson directing *New Toys* with Richard Barthelmess.

Universal Studio, Fort Lee N.J.: George B. Seitz directing *Galloping Hoofs.*

IN EUROPE. Famous Players-Lasky Corp in France: Allan Dwan directing *The Coast of Folly* with Gloria Swanson. . . Metro-Goldwyn Corp in Rome: Fred Niblo directing *Ben Hur* with Ramon Novarro, May McAvoy, Francis X. Bushman. In France: Rex Ingram soon begins directing *Mare Nostrum* with Antonio Moreno and Alice Terry.

CHANGES IN TITLES. FBO Productions: Harry Garson Production originally titled *The Forgotten City* and later changed to *The Stranger from Nowhere* will be released as *The Millionaire Cowboy.*

Universal Productions: *Jazz Parents* will be released as *The Mad Whirl. The Flower of Napoli* is now *The Fighting Cop. Ann's an Idiot* will be released as *Dangerous Innocence.*

United Artists: D.W.Griffith Production, *Dawn*, will be released as *Isn't Life Wonderful.*

Appendix B
Titles and Directors of Films Reviewed in Volumes 1 to 5

THE FIRST TYCOONS

The Squaw Man. Cecil B. DeMille/Oscar Apfel.
The Covered Wagon. James Cruze.

THE FIRST FILM MAKERS

The Italian. Thomas Ince/Reginald Barker.
The Bargain. William S. Hart. The Birth of a Nation. D.W. Griffith.
Intolerance. D.W. Griffith.
Broken Blossoms. D.W. Griffith.
Way Down East. D.W. Griffith.
Lady of the Pavements. D.W. Griffith.
Isn't Life Wonderful. D.W. Griffith.
Foolish Wives. Erich von Stroheim.
Greed. Erich von Stroheim.
The Wedding March. Erich von Stroheim.

THE STARS APPEAR

Panthea. Allan Dwan. [Norma Talmadge]
Excuse My Dust. Sam Wood. [Wallace Reid]
A Poor Little Rich Girl. Maurice Tourneur. [Mary Pickford]
Stella Maris. Marshall Neilan. [Mary Pickford]
Wild and Woolly/The Mollycoddle. [Douglas Fairbanks]
The Thief of Bagdad. Raoul Walsh. [Douglas Fairbanks]
Manhandled. Allan Dwan. [Gloria Swanson]
The Four Horsemen of the Apocalypse. Rex Ingram. [Rudolph Valentino]
The Son of the Sheik. George Fitzmaurice. [Rudolph Valentino]
The Great K and A Train Robbery. Lewis Seiler. [Tom Mix]
The Coward. Reginald Barker. [Charles Ray]
Flesh and the Devil. Clarence Brown. [John Gilbert, Garbo]

THE SILENT COMEDIANS

The Gold Rush. Charlie Chaplin.
Sherlock Jr. Buster Keaton.
Grandma's Boy. Fred Newmeyer. [Harold Lloyd]
Safety Last. Fred Newmeyer, Sam Taylor. [Harold Lloyd]
The Kid Brother. Ted Wilde. [Harold Lloyd]

FILMS OF THE 1920S

Tol'able David. Henry King. [Richard Barthelmess]
Miss Lulu Bett. William deMille.
Manslaughter. Cecil B. DeMille.
The Marriage Circle. Ernst Lubitsch. [Florence Vidor]
Dancing Mothers. Herbert Brenon. [Clara Bow, Alice Joyce]
The Grand Duchess and the Waiter. Mal St. Clair.
Seventh Heaven. Frank Borzage. [Charles Farrell]
Sunrise. F.W. Murnau. [Janet Gaynor]
The Crowd. King Vidor.
The Wind. Victor Seastrom (Sjostrom). [Lillian Gish]
Show People. King Vidor. [Marion Davies]

SEE ALSO: In Volume I, Selected Companies of the Silent Period

Brief Biographies of Early Film Executives

In Volume II, Extant Films of Thomas H. Ince [list]

Feature Length Films Directed by D.W. Griffith [synopses]
Feature Length Films Directed by Erich von Stroheim [synopses]
Twenty Notable Directors [brief biographies]

In Volume III, Performers in Silent Films [176 brief biographies]

Chronology of Film Careers

In Volume IV, Silent Feature Films by Four Comedians [list]

Comedy Performers in Silent Films [brief biographies]

Appendix C
Bibliography

Basic books for students of American silent films are:

Kevin Brownlow, *The Parade's Gone By* (1968), interviews with survivors, including a chapter called "Scenario."
William Everson, *American Silent Film* (1978).
Lewis Jacobs, *The Rise of the American Film* (1939).
Richard Griffith, Arthur Mayer, Eileen Bowser, *The Movies* (1957/1984), a valuable picture history.
Richard Dyer MacCann, series on "American Movies: The First Thirty Years": *The First Tycoons* (1987), *The First Film Makers* (1989), *The Stars Appear* (1992), *The Silent Comedians* (1993).
Frank Magill, *Magill's Survey of Cinema: Silent Films* (1982), three volumes of reviews that emphasize story content and historical background.

Other valuable books:

Cecil B. DeMille. *Autobiography*. Prentice-Hall, 1959.
William C. deMille. *Hollywood Saga*. Dutton, 1939.
Raymond Durgnat and Scott Simmon. *King Vidor, American*. Berkeley, University of California Press, 1988.
Phil Koury. *Yes, Mr. DeMille*. G.P.Putnam's Sons, 1959.
Richard Koszarski. *An Evening's Entertainment: The Age of the Silent Feature Picture 1915-1928*. Charles Scribner's Sons 1994.
Graham Petrie. *Hollywood Destinies:European Directors in America, 1922-1931*. Routledge & Kegan Paul, 1985. Chapter on "The Reception of Foreign Films in America, 1920-1927."
David Robinson, *Hollywood in the Twenties*. Tantivy Press, 1968.
Kay Sloan. *The Loud Silents*. University of Illinois Press, 1988. Social problems in early American films.
Adela Rogers St. Johns. *Love, Laughter and Tears: My Hollywood Story*. Doubleday 1978.
King Vidor. *A Tree Is a Tree*. Harcourt Brace 1952. His earliest days at Universal; directing *The Big Parade* and *The Crowd*.

A few lesser known articles:

Anonymous, "How Twelve Famous Women Scenario Writers Succeeded." *Photoplay*, August 1923. Photos of Anita Loos, Frances Marion, Ouida Bergere, June Mathis, Clara Beranger, Jane Murfin, etc.

---------, "The Shadow Stage:the Six Best Pictures of the Month." *A Woman of Paris*, in which "Chaplin has given other directors a post-graduate course."

Brownlow, Kevin, "Sidney A. Franklin." *Focus on Film*, Summer 1972 (No. 10). Life and films of the MGM director-producer.

DeMille, Cecil B., "The Public Is Always Right." *Ladies' Home Journal*, September 1927.

Everson, William K., "Discoveries of the Seventies." *Focus on Film*, October 1980 (No. 36). The search to discover and preserve silent films that may still exist.

Hilliker, Katharine, "Writing the Titles." In *Opportunities in the Motion Picture Industry*. Photoplay Research Society 1922.

Koszarski, Richard, "Maurice Tourneur: The First of the Visual Stylists." *Film Comment*, March 1973 (Vol. 9, No. 2).

Lounsbury, Myron, "Flashes of Lightning: The Moving Picture in the Progressive Era." *Journal of Popular Culture*, Vol. 3, No. 4, 1970.

McVay, Douglas, "Lubitsch:The American Silent Films." *Focus on Film*, April 1979 (No. 32).

Quirk, James, "Moral House-Cleaning in Hollywood. An Open Letter to Mr. Will Hays." *Photoplay*, April 1923.

Smith, Frederick James, "Foolish Censors." *Photoplay*, October 1922, pp. 39-41, 106. What state censors have clipped out.

St.Johns, Adela Rogers and Katherine Hilliker, "The Motion Picture Alibi." *Photoplay*, March 1922. Examples of written titles that bridged plot problems, etc.

-------, "Just Mickey." *Photoplay*, March 1923. Biography and evaluation of American director, Marshall Neilan.

St.Johns, Ivan, "Marion Fairfax, One of Few Women Producers." *Photoplay*, August 1926.

Staiger, Janet, "Class, ethnicity, and Gender: Explaining the Development of Early American Film Narrative." *Iris*, No. 11.

Valentine, Sydney, "The Girl Producer." *Photoplay*, July 1923. Grace Haskins has written and directed a picture at age 22.

Waterbury, Ruth, "Sex—With a Sense of Humor." *Photoplay*, September 1926. About the director Malcolm St. Clair.

Index

[This index does not cover footnotes, cast lists, filmographies, lists of names or titles, acknowledgments, the contents page, or the appendices.]

Film Titles

About the Author

Richard Dyer MacCann (A.B., University of Kansas; M.A., Stanford University; Ph.D., Harvard University) is Emeritus Professor of Motion Picture History at the University of Iowa, where he taught from 1970 to 1986 and part time in 1987 and 1988. His degrees were all in political science, but he spent most of his career as a professor of film studies. His dissertation on U.S. government documentary films (published by Hastings House in 1973 as *The People's Films*) led him to a position as staff correspondent for the *Christian Science Monitor* in Hollywood and Los Angeles from 1951 to 1957. He has taught film writing, documentary film, and American motion picture history at the University of Southern California and the University of Kansas.

Dr. MacCann was founding editor of *Cinema Journal* for the Society for Cinema Studies (1967 to 1976) and is Distinguished Life Member of the University Film and Video Association. He was State Department film adviser to the Republic of Korea in 1963 and was awarded the first Senior Fellowship in film by the National Endowment for the Humanities for study in London in 1973. He is the author of 40 published articles and 12 books, including *Hollywood in Transition* (Houghton Mifflin, 1962), *Film and Society* (Scribners, 1964), *Film: A Montage of Theories* (Dutton, 1966), *The New Film Index* (Dutton, 1975). He has produced five film works and two video series, including 12 illustrated lectures coordinate with the titles of the books — notably *The First Film Makers* (1989) and *The Stars Appear* (1992) — in this Scarecrow Press series. His most recent book is *A New Vice Presidency for a New Century* (Image & Idea, 1991).